brunch party

PARTY COOKBOOK

kitchen tea

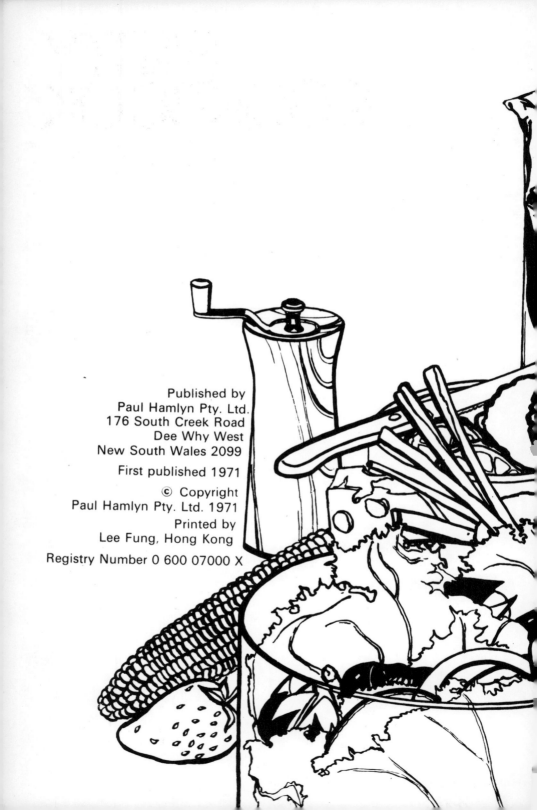

Published by
Paul Hamlyn Pty. Ltd.
176 South Creek Road
Dee Why West
New South Wales 2099

First published 1971

© Copyright
Paul Hamlyn Pty. Ltd. 1971

Printed by
Lee Fung, Hong Kong

Registry Number 0 600 07000 X

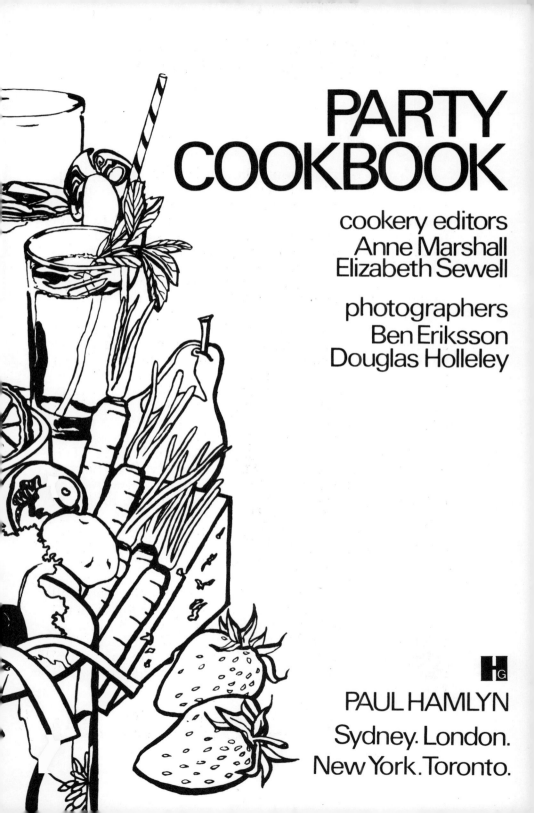

PARTY COOKBOOK

cookery editors
Anne Marshall
Elizabeth Sewell

photographers
Ben Eriksson
Douglas Holleley

HG

PAUL HAMLYN

Sydney. London.
New York. Toronto.

INTRODUCTION

Giving parties should be fun! Here we have the Party Cookbook. Following the great success of the Australian and New Zealand Complete Book of Cookery, which contained exciting new recipes submitted by leading food and wine experts in both countries, we decided to devote a book completely to the art of giving parties and again collected ideas from some more cookery experts, who are also keen party givers. They give you their valuable opinions on suitable food to serve on various occasions.

We have all been confronted with the task of planning a menu for a party being given for a special occasion—a kitchen tea for a close friend, a casual buffet for a larger group of people or a formal dinner party for relations. What should you eat and how does one plan the work beforehand? In this book we have compiled delicious menus suitable for a particular occasion. These menus are easy to prepare and are decidedly different.

What could be more fun than a brunch party? This is an ideal way to entertain friends casually. Why not ask a few friends home for supper after the theatre, or why not have 'open house'? There are innumerable ideas and they are all great fun. The hostess should be able to relax while entertaining friends, so learn to organise your work and then enjoy the party. There are timetables which are easy to follow and are indispensible if one is to be a relaxed hostess.

Do not attempt too much. Write shopping lists well in advance, select suitable china and linen, cook as much as possible beforehand and do not overwork on the day of the party. Informality is the keynote to success.

I hope the Party Cookbook will give you many new ideas and will encourage you to open your doors and welcome your friends.

Elizabeth Sewell

CONTENTS

WEIGHTS AND MEASURES

The weights and fluid measures used throughout this book refer to those of THE STANDARDS ASSOCIATION OF AUSTRALIA. All spoon measurements are level unless otherwise stated. When a recipe calls for a 'good' tablespoon, measure generously. For a 'scant' tablespoon, measure conservatively. A good set of scales, a graduated Australian Standard measuring cup and a set of Australian Standard measuring spoons will be most helpful. These are available at leading hardware stores.

The Australian Standard measuring cup has a capacity of 8 fluid ounces.
The Australian Standard tablespoon has a capacity of 20 millilitres.
The Australian Standard teaspoon has a capacity of 5 millilitres.
The British Imperial pint (used in Australia and in this book) has a volume of 20 fluid ounces.

IMPORTANT WEIGHTS AND MEASURES

AMERICAN weights and measures are the same except for the tablespoon and the pint.
Housewives in AMERICA and CANADA using this book should remember that the AUSTRALIAN standard measuring tablespoon has a capacity of 20 millilitres, whereas the AMERICAN/CANADIAN standard measuring tablespoon has a capacity of 15 millilitres, therefore all tablespoon measures should

be taken generously in AMERICA and CANADA.
It is also important to know that the Imperial pint
(20 fluid ounces) is used in AUSTRALIA and in this
book, whereas the AMERICAN/CANADIAN pint
is 16 fluid ounces.

e.g.

1 Australian pint.............................. $2\frac{1}{2}$ cups
$\frac{1}{2}$ Australian pint.............................. $1\frac{1}{4}$ cups
$\frac{1}{4}$ Australian pint.............................. 5 fluid ounces

OVEN TEMPERATURES

This is an approximate guide only. Different makes of
stoves vary and even the same make of stove can
give slightly different individual results at the same
temperature. If in doubt with your particular stove,
do refer to your own manufacturer's temperature chart.
It is impossible in a general book to be exact for every
stove, but the following is a good average guide in
every case.

Description of Oven	Automatic Electric	Gas Thermostat Setting °F
Cool or low	200	200
Very slow	250	250
Slow	300–325	300
Moderately slow	325–350	325
Moderate	350–375	350
Moderately hot	375–400	375
Hot	400–450	400
Very hot	450–500	450

BRUNCH PARTY

Anne Whitehead

What could be more fun than collecting your friends around you and having a leisurely Brunch Party. It is an ideal way of entertaining weekend guests or friends during vacation time. All the family will enjoy themselves and the atmosphere will be relaxed and gay. The children can help carry things out of doors if the weather is fine. We have an ideal climate for outdoor living. Ask your guests to dress casually and arrive late in the morning. A variety of food may be served. We have such an abundance of wonderful primary products to choose from—meat, milk, eggs, fish and fruit.

For a substantial Brunch Party, start the day with freshly squeezed fruit juice, served chilled in tall glasses. Prepare a large bowl of fresh fruit salad combining two or three fruits in season and serve with a jug of cream. Choose a hearty main dish to follow—Scrambled Eggs and Tomatoes or Liver and Onions with Bacon. Serve plenty of hot buttered toast, croissants or freshly baked scones and a selection of tasty marmalades, jams or honey. Make sure you have a good supply of freshly made tea and percolated coffee. If you prefer a Continental style breakfast, serve fruit juice followed by buttered Cinnamon Nut Bun (see page 15) and large cups of steaming hot coffee. Set the table, using your gayest linen and china and ask your guests to help themselves. Prepare as much as possible in advance and when the guests arrive, relax and enjoy their company, it is a wonderful way to entertain.

BRUNCH MUSHROOMS

Time: 5–10 minutes
Serves: 6–8

To Fry Mushrooms: Drain after washing. Heat some clarified dripping in a large frypan. Have it only a little hotter than for eggs, carefully put in the mushrooms topside down. Sprinkle fins lightly with salt and pepper. Fry gently until the stem centre is tender, turn and fry for a minute or two on the other side before serving. Mushrooms shrink while cooking, never fry too quickly or they will toughen and the edges will become crisp. Serve with fried or grilled steak or chops.

To Stew Mushrooms: To each 1 lb mushrooms allow 1 oz butter, salt and pepper, 1 tablespoon cornflour and 1 cup milk. After cleaning and washing mushrooms, slice them into a saucepan and add the butter and salt and pepper. Put lid on and simmer gently until mushrooms are tender. This may take from 20-30 minutes. Blend cornflour with the milk and pour into the mushrooms, stirring continuously until boiling. Boil for 3 minutes. Adjust seasoning and serve hot with fried or grilled steak or chops.

LAMB CUTLETS WITH TOMATOES

Time: 15 minutes
Temperature: 360°F
Serves: 4

8 lamb cutlets (1–1½ lb)   2 tomatoes
1 teaspoon butter

Preheat electric frypan. Trim cutlets of excess fat along the stem of the bone. Grease frypan surface with butter to prevent the cutlets sticking while cooking. Place cutlets in frypan. Cook for 5 minutes on each side. No extra fat need be added as the cutlets contain a high proportion and will cook in their own fat. When cooked, place cutlets on a heated serving dish and keep warm. Wash and halve tomatoes. Fry until a golden brown on both sides in the same pan. Serve hot with cutlets.

LIVER AND ONIONS WITH BACON

Time: **15 minutes**
Serves: **4–6**

1 sheep's liver
8 oz bacon rashers
clarified dripping
3 onions, thinly sliced

plain flour
pepper
parsley sprigs, for garnish

Thoroughly clean and wash the liver. Remove the skin and slice thinly discarding the parts with a lot of blood vessels. Remove rind from bacon, cut each rasher into 2 or 3 pieces and dry fry in a heated frying pan. Place on absorbent paper in oven to keep hot. Add a little dripping to pan if necessary and gently fry the onions until golden brown. Remove from pan, drain and keep hot with bacon. Fry the liver moderately quickly allowing about 3 minutes on each side. Drain and keep hot with the bacon and onions in the oven. Make a little gravy with the pan drippings, a sprinkling of plain flour, pepper and water. Taste and add salt if necessary. Serve liver, onions and bacon garnished with small sprigs of parsley.

SCRAMBLED EGGS AND TOMATOES

Time: **10 minutes**

allow 2 eggs and 1 tomato
  per person

butter
salt and pepper

Beat the eggs slightly. Skin and slice tomato and cook gently in butter with salt and pepper, until tender. Pour eggs into tomatoes and stir over gentle heat until the mixture is lightly set. Serve with hot buttered toast.

10

POTATO GIRDLE SCONES

Time: 10 minutes
Yield: 8-12

1–2 cups mashed potatoes   **salt and pepper**
1–2 oz butter   **self-raising flour**

Cook the potatoes in the morning or use some from the previous evening's meal. Mix in the butter and salt and pepper. If potatoes are from the night before, melt the butter to mix it in more readily. Work in as much self-raising flour as necessary to make a good scone dough. Press into a round about $\frac{1}{4}$-inch thick, on a floured board. Cut into 8-12 wedges, rounds or squares. Cook on a heated, lightly greased griddle or in a heavy based frying pan, allowing approximately 5 minutes each side until cooked through and a deep golden brown. These are often turned on their sides to get a crisp golden finish all around and to make certain the centre is well done. Serve piping hot with fried eggs and bacon, poached eggs, fried or grilled tomatoes or mushrooms, or split and butter them and serve with honey.

SAVOURY MINCE ON TOAST

Time: 20–25 minutes
Serves: 4

1 tablespoon onion, finely
   chopped
2 oz butter
12 oz minced beef
½ teaspoon salt

1 cup water
1 good tablespoon (½ oz)
   plain flour
4 toast triangles, buttered
4 slices tomato

Cook onion in butter in a saucepan until transparent but not brown. Add minced beef and break it up as it cooks in the butter, using a wooden spatula or spoon. Add salt. When minced meat is brown, pour in nearly all the water and bring to boiling point. Reduce heat and simmer 10 minutes. Make flour into a paste with remaining water and thicken mince with it, stirring continuously. Cook for 5 minutes, reducing the volume of liquid to a binding consistency. Serve hot mince on buttered toast with a slice of tomato.

SMOKED FISH CAKES

Time: 35 minutes
Temperature: 360°F in electric frypan
Serves: 4–6

12 oz smoked cod	2 tablespoons finely
8 oz potatoes	chopped celery
½ teaspoon salt	2 eggs
freshly ground white	3 tablespoons dry bread-
pepper	crumbs
1 oz butter	2–3 oz butter, for frying
1 tablespoon finely	lemon and parsley sprigs,
chopped onion	for garnish

To Prepare Fish and Potatoes: Most convenient when prepared the night before to halve preparation time in the morning. Cut cod into chunks. Place in the top section of a steamer. Peel and slice potatoes. Place in boiling salted water in a saucepan. Place steamer section on top, cover and cook over a medium heat for 20 minutes. Drain potatoes and mash, seasoning with salt and white pepper. Add butter, onion, celery and 1 beaten egg, mix thoroughly. Flake cod and remove all bones.

To Make Fishcakes: Preheat electric frypan. Combine flaked cod, mashed potato mixture, adding a little milk if the mixture is too dry. Shape, forming round cakes approximately ½-inch thick. Dip in the remaining egg which has been beaten slightly. Coat with breadcrumbs. Melt butter in frypan. Cook fish cakes until a crisp golden brown on both sides. Serve hot, garnished with lemon and parsley.

MORNING COFFEE PARTY

Enid Wells

A Morning Coffee Party should be casual and easy to prepare. It is an ideal way to entertain a group of friends. It is also a good way to hold a committee meeting or to raise money for a charity. Make sure the coffee is piping hot and freshly made, it may be served in a variety of ways. Percolated coffee is preferred by most people. Instant coffee is favoured by some because of the short preparation time. For a Morning Coffee Party, the hostess should be prepared to serve percolated coffee—black or with cream or heated milk, or in summer, iced coffee with whipped cream. The food should be simple, varied in flavour, attractively presented but never elaborately decorated. Buttered buns or fruit loaves, biscuits and plain butter cakes are ideal. The table setting should be bright. Colour can be introduced with serviettes and a small flower arrangement. The china should be fine but plain.

Guide to Quantities:
1 pint coffee fills 3 tea cups (average tea cup size). These are generally used for morning coffee.

MENU
Cinnamon Nut Bun
Cheese Roughs
Gingerbread
Coffee Cake
Coffee

CINNAMON NUT BUN

Time: 20–25 minutes
Temperature: 375–400°F
Serves: 12–16

Bun dough:
1 oz compressed yeast
1 teaspoon sugar
1 teaspoon plain flour
1 cup warm milk
2 oz butter

3 cups (12 oz) plain flour
1 teaspoon salt
1 egg
½ cup (4 oz) sugar
½ tablet (5 mg) ascorbic
  acid

For filling:
2 oz butter
2 teaspoons ground
  cinnamon
4 tablespoons desiccated
  coconut

2 teaspoons cocoa
2 tablespoons (1 oz) castor
  sugar
4 teaspoons brandy
1 teaspoon vanilla or
  almond essence

For topping:
4 oz pure icing sugar
warm water

few drops vanilla essence
2 oz grated macadamia
  nuts or toasted almonds

To Make Bun Dough: Mix crumbled yeast, teaspoon of
sugar and flour with the warm milk. Stand for 10
minutes in a warm place. Rub butter into the sieved
flour and salt. Beat the egg with 4 oz sugar. Add the
crushed ascorbic acid to the milk mixture then add to
the beaten egg and sugar. Pour the liquid into a well
in the flour and work with a wooden spoon to a smooth
dough. Beat until dough becomes smooth and resistant.
Turn onto a lightly floured board, knead for
10 minutes. Place in a warm greased bowl, cover with a
clean tea towel or clear plastic and stand in a warm
place for approximately 40 minutes or until the dough
has doubled in bulk. Turn onto a board, knead well,
cut into two equal portions. Roll into rectangles
18 × 3-inches. Spread centre strips with butter,
cinnamon, coconut, cocoa and castor sugar, sprinkle
with brandy and essence and roll up lengthways,
pinching edges firmly together. Grease two 7-inch
sandwich tins and coil a roll into each. Cover with a
clean tea towel or clear plastic, stand in a warm place
for 10-15 minutes or until twice its size. Bake in a
moderately hot oven for 20-25 minutes. Turn onto a
wire cooling tray. While still warm, spread buns
with thin icing, made by mixing sieved icing sugar with
sufficient warm water and the vanilla essence to make a
spreading consistency. Sprinkle with nuts.

15

CHEESE ROUGHS

Time: 15–20 minutes
Temperature: 325–350°F
Serves: 16

1 cup (4 oz) self-raising
  flour
1 teaspoon salt
½ teaspoon pepper or pinch
  of cayenne pepper

4 oz butter or margarine
2 oz mature tasty cheese,
  grated
3–4 oz desiccated coconut

Sift dry ingredients into a mixing bowl and rub in the butter. Add the cheese and mix to a dry dough. Take small portions and roll into even sized balls. Toss in coconut, place on a greased baking tray and bake in a moderately slow oven for 15-20 minutes. Cool on a wire cooling tray.

GINGERBREAD

Time: 45–50 minutes
Temperature: 350–375°F
Serves: 16

4 oz butter
⅔ cup (4 oz) brown sugar
1 egg
4 tablespoons treacle
1½ cups (6 oz) plain flour
1 tablespoon ground ginger
1 teaspoon ground
  cinnamon

½ cup milk
1 teaspoon bicarbonate of
  soda, dissolved in 2
  tablespoons boiling
  water
2 tablespoons chopped
  preserved ginger

For icing: (optional)
4 oz pure icing sugar

juice of ½ lemon
warm water or milk

Cream butter and brown sugar in a mixing bowl, add beaten egg and beat well. Add the treacle. Add the sieved dry ingredients alternately with the milk. Lastly add soda and boiling water and the chopped ginger. Pour into a 7-inch square cake tin, lined with well greased greaseproof paper. Bake in a moderate oven for 45-50 minutes. Turn onto a wire cooling tray to cool. To Make Icing: Mix sieved icing sugar with lemon juice and sufficient warm water or milk to make a smooth spreading consistency. Ice Gingerbread when cool.

16

COFFEE CAKE

Time: 30 minutes
Temperature: 350–375°F
Serves: 16

4 oz butter or margarine
1 scant cup (6 oz) castor
  sugar
1 egg
$\frac{1}{2}$ teaspoon vanilla essence
2 cups (8 oz) self-raising
  flour

Topping:
$\frac{2}{3}$ cup (4 oz) brown sugar
2–3 oz chopped walnuts
2 good tablespoons (1 oz)
  plain flour

$\frac{1}{2}$ teaspoon salt
$\frac{3}{4}$ cup milk
2 tablespoons golden syrup
1 teaspoon ground
  cinnamon
$\frac{1}{4}$ teaspoon ground nutmeg
$\frac{1}{4}$ teaspoon ground cloves
$\frac{1}{2}$ teaspoon ground
  cinnamon
2 oz butter

Cream the butter and castor sugar in a mixing bowl
until light and fluffy. Add the egg and beat well, then
add the vanilla essence. Sift the flour and salt together,
add to the creamed mixture alternately with the milk.
Divide mixture into two equal parts. To one part add
the golden syrup and spices. Spoon mixtures
alternately into a 9-inch square cake tin, lined with
greased greaseproof paper. Zig-zag a spatula through
the mixture to give a marbled effect. Sprinkle with
topping and bake in a moderate oven for 30 minutes.
When cool, cut into squares.

To Make Topping: Put the brown sugar, walnuts,
flour and cinnamon into a bowl, add melted butter
and mix well.

luncheon party

LUNCHEON PARTY

Elah Lowe

The following menu is suitable for a special person one has invited to lunch, for any group with a guest speaker, or for a party of friends. The luncheon suggested is light and interesting and can be prepared in advance, which is essential for the hostess who can then be with her guests. She can be relaxed and entertaining, rather than hot and flustered, in the kitchen.

MENU
Chicken Cacciatora
Noodles
Pears Vinaigrette
Cheese
Malakoff

Day Before:
Make Malakoff.
Make mint vinaigrette dressing.
Prepare chicken and fry until golden, for Chicken Cacciatora.
Prepare tomato sauce, and pour over chicken in casserole.
Cover, cool and place in refrigerator.
Timetable:
10.00 a.m. Chill wine.
12.00 noon Prepare pears, arrange on lettuce on a serving plate, cover with mint vinaigrette dressing. Cover with clear plastic and chill in refrigerator.
12.15 p.m. Put Chicken Cacciatora in a moderate oven to cook.
Set table.
12.30 p.m. Prepare cheese board.
Put noodles on to boil.
 1.00 p.m. Drain noodles. Serve Chicken Cacciatora.

18

CHICKEN CACCIATORA

Time: 40 minutes
Temperature: 350–375°F
Serves: 6

2 x 2½ lb roasting chickens
½ cup (2 oz) plain flour
pepper
2 tablespoons olive oil
1 oz butter
1 green capsicum, diced
1 white onion, chopped
2 cloves garlic, finely
  chopped
1 carrot, diced

3 cups tomatoes, skinned
  (tinned tomatoes may be
  used)
1 bay leaf
salt and pepper
2 tablespoons sherry
1 tablespoon chopped
  parsley,
6 black olives and 6 green
  olives, for garnish

Cut chicken into serving pieces. Wipe and dip chicken pieces into seasoned flour. Heat oil and butter in a heavy based frying pan and fry chicken until golden brown on all sides. Remove chicken from pan and keep warm in a large heavy based saucepan or flameproof casserole. Fry green capsicum, onion, garlic and carrot in frying pan, adding a little extra oil if necessary. Cook until onion is soft and golden. Add tomatoes. If tinned tomatoes are used, drain liquid off first. Add bay leaf and salt and pepper to taste. Bring to boil, simmer a few minutes, then pour sauce over chicken pieces. Add sherry. Cover and simmer gently on top of stove or cook in a moderate oven for about 30 minutes or until chicken is tender. Garnish chicken with chopped parsley and spiral cut olives. Serve with boiled noodles.

PEARS VINAIGRETTE

Serves: 6

6 ripe dessert pears

For mint vinaigrette
   dressing:
6 tablespoons olive oil
3 tablespoons wine vinegar
2 tablespoons chopped
   mint
2 tablespoons chopped
   parsley

salt
freshly ground black
   pepper
$\frac{1}{2}$ teaspoon dry mustard
lettuce, for garnish

Peel pears thinly, cut in halves, remove cores. Arrange
on lettuce on a serving plate.
To Make Dressing: Combine olive oil, vinegar, mint
and parsley in a mixing bowl. Season to taste with salt,
freshly ground black pepper and dry mustard. Mix well.
Pour mint vinaigrette dressing over pears and chill
before serving.
Note: Tinned pears may be served in this way when
fresh pears are out of season.

MALAKOFF

Serves: 6

6 oz ground almonds
½ good cup (4 oz) castor sugar
¾ cup cream
6 oz unsalted butter
3 egg yolks
2 tablespoons rum

12 oz plain sweet biscuits
1 cup cream flavoured with 1 tablespoon rum
extra ½ pint cream, whipped
extra 2 tablespoons rum
toasted almonds, for decoration

Mix ground almonds, castor sugar, ¾ cup cream, melted butter and egg yolks together with 2 tablespoons rum. Dip biscuits into cream flavoured with rum and place on a serving dish. Cover with almond mixture then another layer of dipped biscuits and so on until all ingredients are used, finishing with a layer of biscuits. Cover with whipped cream, flavoured with extra rum. Place in refrigerator for at least 8 hours, preferably overnight. Before serving, top with toasted almonds.

KITCHEN TEA
.Rosemary Thurston

A Kitchen Tea is given for a bride to be. A very feminine occasion when dainty morsels of savoury and sweet food are served on pretty china. As a guide to tea-making, remember that 4 oz tea makes 20 cups.

MENU
Pineapple Punch
Fish Patties
Savoury Eggs
Fruit Meringues
Chocolate Rum Truffles
Tea

Two Days Before:
Make Chocolate Rum Truffles, store in an air-tight
container, in refrigerator.
Day Before:
Make meringues, store in an air-tight container.
Hard-boil eggs.
Wash and dry lettuce, place in refrigerator in an
air-tight container.
Make sauce for Fish Patties, cover with wet greaseproof
paper and refrigerate.
Make flaky pastry, roll and fold, wrap in plastic and
refrigerate.
Morning:
Cook smoked fish, flake and mix with sauce.
Roll out pastry, make Fish Patties and bake.
Make syrup for Pineapple Punch, mix with fruit juice
and chill. Make Savoury Eggs, arrange on lettuce on a
serving plate. Cover with clear plastic and place in
refrigerator. Prepare fruit for Fruit Meringues.
Timetable:
2.30 p.m. Set table.
2.45 p.m. Reheat Fish Patties in a moderate oven.
3.00 p.m. Whip cream and assemble Fruit Meringues.
3.30 p.m. Add ginger ale and ice cubes to Pineapple
Punch.
Serve Kitchen Tea.

PINEAPPLE PUNCH

Serves: 12

3 cups water
2 cups (1 lb) sugar
1 x 30 oz tin pineapple juice
½ cup lemon juice

3 large bottles dry ginger
ale
ice cubes

Measure water and sugar into a saucepan and bring to
the boil. In a large bowl, mix pineapple and lemon
juice. Pour the hot syrup over the juices, chill. Just
before serving, add dry ginger ale and ice cubes.

FISH PATTIES

Time: 12–15 minutes
Temperature: 400–450°F
Yield: 24

2 oz butter
3 good tablespoons ($1\frac{1}{2}$ oz)
  plain flour
1 pint milk
12 oz smoked fish, finely
  flaked
$\frac{1}{4}$ cup lemon juice

$\frac{1}{4}$ cup finely chopped
  parsley
salt
cayenne pepper
1 lb flaky pastry (see
  page 38)

In a medium sized saucepan, melt the butter. Add flour and mix until smooth. Blend in the milk, return to heat and stirring continuously, bring to the boil. Cook for 2 minutes, cool and cover. Mix in the fish, lemon juice and parsley. Season to taste with salt and cayenne pepper. Roll pastry out thinly. With a cutter, cut into small circles and line 24 patty tins. Place cold fish mixture into the pastry cases. Bake in a hot oven for 12-15 minutes and serve immediately. If Fish Patties are cooked in advance, before serving, place in a moderate oven (350-375°F) and heat for 10-15 minutes.

SAVOURY EGGS

Yield: 24

12 hard-boiled eggs
1 oz butter
3 tablespoons grated onion
1 teaspoon curry powder
1 teaspoon sugar
2 tablespoons tomato sauce
2 tablespoons finely
  chopped parsley

approximately $\frac{1}{4}$ cup top of
  milk or cream
salt and pepper
24 small lettuce cups or
  several lettuce leaves

Shell the hard-boiled eggs and cut lengthways. Scoop out the yolks and place in a small bowl, add the butter and mash together to form a smooth paste. Mix in the onion, curry powder, sugar, tomato sauce and parsley. Mix with enough top of milk or cream to make a smooth, thick paste. Add salt and pepper to taste. Pile mixture into reserved egg whites. Arrange in small lettuce cups or on a bed of lettuce leaves.

FRUIT MERINGUES

Time: 1 hour
Temperature: 250°F
Yield: 24–30

2 egg whites
½ good cup (4 oz) castor
  sugar
1 cup cream, whipped

fruit such as pineapple,
Chinese gooseberries,
  strawberries or other
  firm, acid fruits

Set oven at very slow and place shelves near centre.
Cover 2 baking trays with waxed paper, shiny side up,
or greased greaseproof paper. Whisk egg whites until
stiff, beat in sugar a tablespoon at a time and continue
beating until the mixture is stiff. Using a forcing bag
with a smooth ½-inch pipe or 2 spoons, shape mixture
in small rounds on baking trays. Make a depression
in the centre of each meringue with the back of a
teaspoon. Turn oven off and place meringues inside.
Leave in oven for 1 hour or until dry right through.
Remove from paper and allow to cool before storing in
an air-tight container.
Before serving, top each meringue with whipped cream
and a piece of fruit.

CHOCOLATE RUM TRUFFLES

Yield: 72

8 oz water biscuits
8 oz butter
4 oz cocoa
4 oz desiccated coconut
12 oz icing sugar

2 tablespoons rum
6 tablespoons sherry
extra coconut or
  chocolate vermicelli

Crush biscuits finely. In a medium sized saucepan,
melt the butter. Mix in the cocoa, coconut and icing
sugar. Add crushed biscuits and blend well. Stir in
rum, add sherry a tablespoon at a time until the mixture
binds together. It may be necessary to add more sherry
if the mixture is too dry. Roll the mixture into small
balls ½-inch in diameter and roll in the extra coconut or
chocolate vermicelli. Store in an air-tight container
in the refrigerator.
Note: Chocolate Rum Truffles will keep for weeks in
the refrigerator.

CHRISTENING TEA

Kay Madigan

A Christening Tea is a very special occasion, here is a menu which is simple but tasty and may be prepared in advance.

MENU
Ham and Shrimp Puffs
Ribbon Sandwiches
Mixed Tartlets
Ginger Cream Cakes
Almond Roll
Christening Cake

Six Weeks Before:
Make Christening Cake, wrap and secure in an air-tight container.

One Week Before:
Cover Christening Cake with Almond Paste.

Two Days Before:
Cover Christening Cake with Fondant Paste and complete decoration of cake.

One Day Before:
Make and bake pastry tartlets and prepare the 3 unbaked fillings.
Make ginger cakes.
Make Ribbon Sandwiches, wrap in aluminium foil or clear plastic and place in refrigerator.
Prepare fillings for Ham and Shrimp Puffs, cover with wet greaseproof paper and refrigerate.
Assemble ingredients for choux pastry cases and Almond Roll.

Morning:
Make and bake choux pastry cases.
Make sponge for Almond Roll, cool, fill and roll up.
Fill baked pastry tartlets with the 3 prepared fillings.
Fill choux pastry cases with ham and shrimp fillings.

Timetable:
2.00 p.m. Set table.
3.00 p.m. Christening.
3.45 p.m. Reheat Ham and Shrimp Puffs in a slow oven.
Whip cream and decorate Mixed Tartlets, Ginger Cream Cakes and Almond Roll.
Remove crusts from sandwiches and arrange on plates.
4.00 p.m. Serve Christening Tea.

27

HAM AND SHRIMP PUFFS

Time: 20 minutes
Temperature: 400–450°F
Yield: 18

Choux pastry cases:
½ pint water
4 oz butter or margarine

1¼ cups (5 oz) plain flour
4 eggs
salt and pepper

For fillings:
Ham:
½ pint White Sauce (see page 29)
½ green capsicum, chopped
1 chicken stock cube, crumbled

8 oz cooked ham, chopped
salt and pepper

Shrimp:
½ pint White Sauce (see page 29)
1 x 6½ oz tin shrimps
2 oz grated cheese

2 spring onions, chopped
1 tablespoon chopped parsley
salt and pepper

To Make Choux Pastry Cases: Place the water and butter into a saucepan over a medium heat. Sieve the flour onto a piece of greaseproof paper. When the water is boiling and butter dissolves, quickly pour the flour into the saucepan, stirring rapidly with a wooden spoon. Continue stirring until the mixture forms a smooth soft ball and leaves the sides of the saucepan. Remove from heat. Allow to cool for 2 minutes. Beat eggs slightly, add to mixture approximately one at a time and beat well until thoroughly absorbed. Continue to beat in the eggs until a satin-like shine develops. Place teaspoons of the mixture onto a greased baking tray. Bake in a hot oven for 20 minutes or until the cases are firm and dry.

To Make the Fillings: Combine ingredients for each filling, heat and place in the baked choux pastry cases. Warm for a few minutes in a moderate oven before serving. Garnish Ham and Shrimp Puffs with parsley. *Note:* The puffs may also be served cold.

WHITE SAUCE

2 oz butter
4 good tablespoons (2 oz) plain flour

salt and pepper
½ pint milk

Melt butter in a saucepan, stir in flour, add salt and pepper to taste, cook over gentle heat, stirring constantly, for 1-2 minutes or until flour has absorbed all the butter. The roux should not be allowed to colour. When roux has a granular appearance, pour in milk, all at once, and bring to the boil over a medium heat, stirring constantly. Reduce heat and simmer for 1-2 minutes. Taste and adjust seasoning if necessary.

RIBBON SANDWICHES

½ loaf brown bread, thinly sliced
½ loaf white bread, thinly sliced

8 oz butter

For Fillings:
● Veal and Ham: Mix together 2 oz finely chopped cooked veal, 2 oz finely chopped cooked ham, 1 stalk finely chopped celery and 1 chopped hard-boiled egg. Add enough commercial mayonnaise to bind mixture together.
● Bacon and Peanut Butter: Mix together 2 rashers cooked, crumbled bacon, 2 tablespoons peanut butter and 1 large chopped gherkin.
● Curried Egg: Mix together 3 hard-boiled eggs and 1 teaspoon curry powder. Add enough commercial mayonnaise to bind mixture together.
● Ham Paste: 1 × 4½ oz tin commercial ham paste.
Butter 1 slice brown bread on one side. Spread with veal and ham filling. Butter both sides of 1 slice of white bread, place on top of veal and ham filling and spread with bacon filling. Butter both sides of second brown slice of bread. Place on top of bacon filling and spread with curried egg filling. Butter both sides of second white slice of bread and place over curried egg filling and spread with ham paste. Butter one side of brown bread and place on top. Press layers together firmly and wrap the sandwiches in aluminium foil or clear plastic and store in the refrigerator. Before serving, remove the crusts and cut each sandwich into fingers. Arrange on plates to show layers.

MIXED TARTLETS

Time: 10–12 minutes
Temperature: 400–450°F
Yield: 48

Pastry tartlets:
2½ cups (10 oz) plain flour
5 oz butter
4 tablespoons (2 oz) castor
  sugar
2 egg yolks
cold water to mix

For fillings:
Macaroon and raspberry
  jam:
raspberry jam
1 egg white
4 tablespoons (2 oz) castor
  sugar
2 tablespoons desiccated
  coconut

Marshmallow and black-
  currant jelly:
blackcurrant jelly
1 tablespoon gelatine
1 cup (8 oz) sugar
1 cup hot water
few drops vanilla essence
red colouring

Pineapple:
½ oz butter
1 x 15 oz tin crushed
  pineapple
juice of 1 lemon
1 scant tablespoon
  cornflour
1 scant tablespoon custard
  powder
1 egg
¼ pint cream, whipped

Apple and cream:
2 cooking apples
1 tablespoon water
2–4 scant tablespoons
  (1–2 oz) sugar
¼ pint cream, whipped, and
  ground cinnamon, for
  decoration

To Make Pastry Tartlets: Sieve the flour into a chilled
mixing bowl. Add the butter and lightly rub into the
flour with the fingertips. When mixture resembles dry
breadcrumbs, stir in sugar and make a well in the centre.
Add the egg yolks and a little cold water. Mix until
a slightly crumbly, stiff dough is made. Knead the
dough a little, cover with clear plastic, cool and rest for
10 minutes in the refrigerator. Roll out and cut into
rounds with a fluted cutter. Place in greased patty tins
and bake in a hot oven for 10-12 minutes. Keep one tray
of cases unbaked for the Macaroon and raspberry
jam tartlets. Remove and cool on a wire cooling tray.

● Macaroon and Raspberry Jam: Place a teaspoon of raspberry jam in each uncooked tart case. Whisk egg white until stiff. Add castor sugar and beat until smooth. Add the coconut and fold in gently and thoroughly. Spoon into cases on top of the jam and bake in a hot oven for 5-10 minutes or until pale brown.
● Marshmallow and Blackcurrant Jelly: Place a teaspoon of blackcurrant jelly in each uncooked tart case. Dissolve gelatine and sugar in water and boil together for 4 minutes. When cool, add vanilla essence and colour pink with red colouring, beat thoroughly until thick and fluffy. Spoon into tart cases on top of the blackcurrant jelly.
● Pineapple: Combine all ingredients except cream in a saucepan. Stirring continuously, bring to simmering point and cook gently for 2 minutes. Cool filling and place in tart cases and decorate with whipped cream before serving.
● Apple and Cream: Peel, core and slice apples. Place in a saucepan with the water and sugar. Simmer until cooked. Cool and strain. Spoon into tart cases. Decorate with cream and sprinkle with cinnamon before serving.

GINGER CREAM CAKES

Time: 12–15 minutes
Temperature: 350–375°F
Yield: 18–24

4 oz butter
2 scant tablespoons (2 oz) sugar
½ cup golden syrup
2 eggs
2 cups (8 oz) self-raising flour

1 teaspoon ground ginger
4 oz preserved ginger, chopped
pinch of salt
½ pint cream, whipped
icing sugar, for decoration

Melt the butter, sugar and golden syrup together and add beaten eggs. Fold in the sieved flour, ground ginger, preserved ginger and salt. Bake in paper cases in a moderate oven for 12-15 minutes. Allow the cakes to cool. Cut a circle from the top of each cake, using a small, sharp knife. Cut the circles in halves. Place a small quantity of whipped cream onto each cake. Replace the half circles to form butterfly wings on top of the cakes. Sprinkle with sieved icing sugar just before serving.

ALMOND ROLL

Time: 12 minutes
Temperature: 350–375°F

3 eggs
½ good cup (4 oz) castor sugar
1 cup (4 oz) self-raising flour

few drops vanilla essence
2–3 tablespoons milk

For filling:
4 oz butter
½ good cup (4 oz) castor sugar

2 eggs, separated
1 teaspoon almond essence
4 oz ground almonds

For topping:
2 tablespoons rum
1 tablespoon orange juice
½ pint cream, whipped, blended with 1 teaspoon gelatine dissolved in 1 tablespoon water

2 oz slivered almonds, toasted
glacé cherries and angelica, for decoration

Place eggs and sugar into a mixing bowl and beat until very thick, fold in sieved flour, vanilla essence and milk. Pour into a Swiss roll tin lined with greased greaseproof paper and bake in a moderate oven for approximately 12 minutes. Turn out onto greaseproof paper sprinkled with castor sugar. Roll up quickly and leave for 2-3 minutes, unroll and remove paper.

To Make Filling: Cream butter and sugar until light and fluffy, beat in egg yolks. Stir in almond essence and ground almonds. Whisk egg whites until stiff and fold into mixture.

To Assemble Cake: Unroll the sponge and sprinkle with rum and orange juice. Spread with the almond filling, then roll the cake up again. Coat with whipped cream mixed with slivered almonds. Decorate with glacé cherries and angelica.

christening tea

CHRISTENING CAKE

Time: **3 hours**
Temperature: **300–325°F**

8 oz butter
8 oz raisins
8 oz sultanas
8 oz currants
4 oz dates
4 oz almonds
2 oz glacé cherries
1 tablespoon fig jam
1 cup sherry
1 teaspoon vanilla essence
1 teaspoon lemon essence
1 tablespoon chopped
  mixed peel

1 cup (6 oz) brown sugar
3 eggs
1¼ cups (5 oz) plain flour
1¼ cups (5 oz) self-raising
  flour
1 teaspoon bicarbonate of
  soda
1 teaspoon each mixed
  spice, ground nutmeg,
  ground cinnamon and
  ground ginger

Line a deep 8-inch round cake tin with aluminium foil. Set oven temperature at slow. Place in a saucepan the butter, mixed fruit, almonds, cherries, fig jam, sherry, vanilla and lemon essence, mixed peel and brown sugar. Bring to the boil and boil for 3 minutes, cool slightly. Place in a large mixing bowl and beat in eggs. Add remaining dry ingredients previously sieved together. Place mixture into prepared cake tin and bake in a slow oven for approximately 3 hours. Allow to stand in tin for 5-10 minutes before removing from tin. Cool, wrap and store in an air-tight container.

To Decorate Christening Cake: Make up 2 lb of icing sugar into Almond Paste (see page 35) and cover the cake. Make up 2 lb icing sugar into Fondant Paste (see page 34) and cover the cake. Tie a coloured ribbon around the cake and place on a cake board. Make up Royal Icing (see page 35) and pipe a shell edge around the base of the cake. Colour the remaining Fondant Paste in pastel colours. Mould into a tiny cradle and stork, using a thick cocktail stick for the bird's leg and blanched almonds for wings. Cut out flower and leaf shapes in a contrasting colour. Arrange decorations on top of the cake and secure with Royal Icing.

children's birthday party

FONDANT PASTE

1 lb icing sugar
1 teaspoon glycerine
2 small or 1 large egg white
2 oz liquid glucose
extra icing sugar

almond or vanilla essence
food colouring
egg white for glazing
cornflour

Sieve the icing sugar into a bowl. Make a well in the centre and add the glycerine, egg white and glucose which has been heated over boiling water to soften. Stir with a wooden spoon until the mixture is cool, then knead with the hand until all the icing sugar is absorbed. Turn onto a board which has been lightly sprinkled with extra sieved icing sugar, flavour and colour as desired and knead until smooth and pliable. Cover until ready to use.

Brush the Almond Paste covering the cake lightly with egg white. Use a sprinkling of icing sugar or cornflour on the board, roll the Fondant Paste to approximately $\frac{1}{4}$-inch thick and large enough to barely cover the cake. Lift onto the cake by rolling around a large rolling pin and unrolling onto the cake. Sprinkle a little cornflour onto the palms of the hands and smooth the surface and sides, making sure that the edges and/or corners are a good shape. Trim the base with a sharp knife to neaten on the board. Allow to stand for a few days before decorating.

ALMOND PASTE

1 lb icing sugar
4–6 oz ground almonds or
  almond meal
2 small or 1 large egg yolk

2 tablespoons sweet sherry
2–3 teaspoons lemon juice
extra icing sugar
egg white for glazing

Sieve the icing sugar, add the ground almonds and mix well. Add the egg yolks and sherry. Mix to a firm dough with the lemon juice. Turn onto a pastry board which has been sprinkled with the extra sieved icing sugar and knead lightly. Roll out until large enough to cover cake, the paste should be approximately $\frac{1}{4}$-inch thick. Level the surface of the cake and brush away any crumbs. Turn upside down onto a board and brush the cake with lightly beaten egg white. This will enable the paste to stick to the cake. Fill in any cracks or uneven pieces on the cake with scraps of Almond Paste to ensure a level surface and contour. Cover the cake with Almond Paste and mould and smooth into shape, making sure the edges and/or corners are a good shape. Cut away any surplus paste around the base of the cake to neaten the join at the board. Set aside for at least 2 days to become firm.

ROYAL ICING

6–8 oz pure icing sugar
  (amount varies according
  to size of egg white)
1 teaspoon liquid glucose

1 egg white
4 drops of lemon juice
  or 2 drops glacial acetic
  acid

Sieve icing sugar through a fine icing sieve. Melt glucose. Beat egg white slightly using a wooden spoon, gradually add icing sugar, beating well. Add lemon juice and melted glucose and beat until icing remains in a point when the spoon is drawn up from it. The icing should be glossy and stiff by beating, rather than by the addition of extra icing sugar. If white icing is required, add a few drops of washing blue. Cover with a damp cloth until required to prevent icing drying out and crusting.

CHILDREN'S BIRTHDAY PARTY

Yvonne McDougall

Catering for Children's Parties.

When planning a party for the pre-school age group, a topical theme helps when selecting recipes. Children delight in food which resembles familiar characters, particularly if they are connected with current radio and television programmes or a favourite book. The amount of food served and the size of the portions is important. A variety of foods served in small amounts avoids waste. Place baskets of sweets on the table towards the end of the party. Children will enjoy taking them home.

Savoury Food.

There has been a definite swing from sweet to savoury food with children today, although ice cream, jellies, cakes and biscuits still have a place on the party menu. Savoury foods such as sandwiches, cheese savouries, cocktail sausages or the more substantial 'hot dog' are some favourites. Make open sandwiches using hard-boiled eggs, cheese or Continental sausage arranged attractively and garnished with parsley, lettuce, gherkin or pickled onion.

Sweet Food.

Fancy shaped iced biscuits, particularly in the form of animals, meringues, éclairs, brandy snaps, decorated sponge cream cakes and buttered bread with hundreds and thousands, are popular. Sweet food should be served in small portions and should not be too rich.

Jelly and Ice Cream.

Fruit set in jelly, jelly set in orange baskets or in fancy moulds appeal to most toddlers. Fresh fruit salad is also a favourite. These desserts are best served in individual portions. For very young children, a simple dessert such as jelly and ice cream served in a square ice block cone is a good idea as there may be some difficulty in using a spoon.

The Birthday Cake.

The birthday cake should be the main point of interest on the table. For a circus party, decorate the cake with colourful clowns and animals. An ice cream cake may also be a change.

A ZOO PARTY
Sausage Rolls
Open Sandwiches
Ginger Biscuits
Zoo Train Trucks
White Mice in Jelly
'Skippy' Birthday Cake
Crisps and Sweets

SAUSAGE ROLLS

Time: 30 minutes
Temperature: 400–450°F
  reducing to   375–400°F
Yield: 24

Flaky pastry:
2 cups (8 oz) plain flour
pinch of salt

6 oz firm butter
$\frac{1}{2}$ teaspoon lemon juice
cold water to mix

Filling:
1 lb sausage meat

egg for glazing

To Make Pastry: Sieve flour and salt together into a mixing bowl. Divide butter into 4 equal portions. Rub 1 portion into the flour with the fingertips. Using a round bladed knife, mix to a pliable soft dough with lemon juice and cold water. Roll out dough to an oblong, about 12 × 5-inches, keeping edges straight and corners square. Brush off excess flour with a pastry brush. Mark oblong into thirds lightly with a knife. Place a portion of butter on two-thirds of dough in little pieces. Sprinkle lightly with flour and fold bottom third of pastry up over middle third and fold top third down. Press edges lightly together with a rolling pin. Turn dough a quarter turn so folded edges are to right and left. Roll out and fold as before including another portion of the butter. Cover dough with clear plastic and chill for 30 minutes. Roll, fold and include final portion of butter as before. Cover dough and chill again for 30 minutes. Roll and fold once more. Use as required.

Note: Equal quantities of butter and lard may be used instead of all butter. Mix both fats together thoroughly before dividing into 4 portions.

To Make Sausage Rolls: Divide pastry in half. Roll each half into an oblong 3 × 12-inches. Form the sausage meat into 2 rolls, 12-inches long. Lay sausage meat down middle of pastry oblongs. Damp one side of pastry with water, fold pastry over, press edges together firmly. Cut each into 12 pieces. Glaze tops of Sausage Rolls with beaten egg, place on a baking tray and bake in a hot oven for 15 minutes. Reduce oven temperature to moderately hot and bake for a further 10-15 minutes or until golden brown.

GINGER BISCUITS

Time: 15 minutes
Temperature: 350–375°F
Yield: 12–16

4 oz butter
4 tablespoons (2 oz) castor sugar

For topping:
4 oz icing sugar
2 oz butter

1 cup (4 oz) self-raising flour
1 teaspoon ground ginger

2 teaspoons ground ginger
2 teaspoons golden syrup
white icing, for decoration

Cream butter and sugar, gradually add sieved flour and ground ginger and mix well. Press firmly into a greased 8 × 12-inch Swiss roll tin. Bake in a moderate oven for 15 minutes.

To Make Topping: Stir all ingredients in a saucepan over a gentle heat until butter is melted and ingredients are well mixed. Pour over biscuit while still hot. Allow to cool. Cut into desired animal shapes with metal cutters. Pipe eyes and mouths on animals with white icing.

WHITE MICE IN JELLY

Serves: 4

1 packet orange jelly crystals
4 pear halves
4 blanched almonds
8 currants

2 glacé cherries
1 long piece angelica
¼ pint cream, whipped, for decoration (optional)

Make jelly and allow to cool thoroughly. Place pear halves, round side up, in individual glass dishes. Decorate as mice by placing halves of almonds for ears, currants for eyes, halved cherries for noses and angelica for whiskers and tails. Pour over cool jelly carefully and allow to set. Just before serving, stars of cream may be piped around the edges of the dishes. *Variation:* Mice may be set in green jelly and licorice used for whiskers and tails.

ZOO TRAIN TRUCKS

Time: 15 minutes
Temperature: 375–400°F
Yield: approximately 32

4 oz butter
1 cup (4 oz) plain flour
3 eggs
½ good cup (4 oz) castor
   sugar

extra 2 good tablespoons
   (1 oz) plain flour
1 teaspoon baking powder
2–3 drops vanilla essence

For icing:
8 oz icing sugar, sifted
2 tablespoons warm water
food colourings

desiccated coconut
multi-coloured flat sweets

Line an 8 × 12-inch Swiss roll tin with greased
greaseproof paper. Cream butter thoroughly in a
mixing bowl and mix in flour to form a soft, creamy
mixture. Warm if necessary. Beat eggs until frothy,
gradually beat in castor sugar until thick and creamy.
Combine the egg mixture with the creamed butter and
flour. Add extra flour and baking powder sieved
together and vanilla essence. Place mixture in the
prepared cake tin. Bake in the centre of a moderately
hot oven for 15 minutes. Allow to cool and turn out.
When cold, cut into 1½-inch squares and place on a
wire cooling tray.
To Make Icing: Place icing sugar and water in a
saucepan and stir over a gentle heat until mixture is
warm. Divide mixture into several portions and colour
as desired. Pour over squares, make sure there is a
plate underneath to catch drips. When icing is almost
firm, sprinkle sides with coconut and press on sweets
to represent wheels. Decorate tops with sweets and
place on a long plate. Cakes should be gaily coloured
and any butter icing over from the 'Skippy' cake could
be used to pipe stars around edge of trucks. Stand a
toy train near the plate to add extra appeal to the Zoo
Train Trucks.

'SKIPPY' BIRTHDAY CAKE

Time: 40 minutes
Temperature: 350–375°F
Serves: 8

12 oz butter or margarine
2 cups (12 oz) castor sugar
6 eggs
1 teaspoon vanilla essence
4 cups (16 oz) plain flour

4 teaspoons baking powder
½ cup milk
red colouring
1 tablespoon cocoa

For butter icing:
5 oz butter
12 oz icing sugar, sifted
few drops vanilla essence
yellow colouring

4 oz desiccated coconut,
   toasted
2 brown flat sweets
green shredded coconut

For glacé icing:
4 oz icing sugar, sifted

1 tablespoon cocoa
1 tablespoon warm water

Cream butter and sugar together in a mixing bowl until light and fluffy. Gradually add beaten eggs and vanilla essence. Add sieved flour and baking powder alternately with milk, a third at a time. Place one third of mixture in heaped spoonfuls into a 14 × 10-inch cake tin lined with greased greaseproof paper. Divide remaining mixture into two and colour one portion pink, with the red colouring and the other portion chocolate, with the cocoa. Place pink and chocolate mixtures in alternate spoonfuls in tin. Bake in a moderate oven for 40 minutes. Allow cake to cool and cut into desired animal shape using a template (pattern) for the outline. Remaining cake forms a boomerang for the base. Place cake on a suitable cake board.

To Make Butter Icing: Cream butter, add icing sugar gradually and vanilla essence and beat until light and fluffy. Add sufficient yellow colouring to give depth of colour desired. Ice cake and sprinkle with toasted coconut. Use a sweet for the eye and nose. Ice boomerang similarly but place coconut only along sides. Pipe 'SKIPPY' along boomerang.

To Make Glacé Icing: Place icing sugar, cocoa and water into a small saucepan and stir over heat until mixture is warm. Ice cake board and decorate with green coconut to represent grass.

OPEN HOUSE PARTY

Len Evans

Occasionally, there is a need to entertain 60-100 people easily and without any fuss. In my case it is a party on Christmas Day, a party which evolved from my days as a hotel keeper, when, after serving Christmas dinner at lunchtime we sought to entertain ourselves. Obviously after cooking for hundreds of people one did not feel like doing the same for hundreds of guests. Therefore the evolvement of the 'without fuss' buffet. When entertaining large numbers of people informally one provides for their sustenance and refreshment in the easiest and most relaxed way. Thus the 'help yourself' food bar originated.

The next point is that if you plan to simply serve 'help yourself' fare the ingredients must be of the finest possible quality. At our yearly party we provide hundreds of freshly baked rolls, butter, cutting boards, knives and various dressings and condiments. The ingredients are cold roast rump of beef, cold roast Scotch fillet, caraway pork neck (a European cut of pork smeared with olive oil, rolled in caraway seeds and gently roasted), Polish salami, Hungarian salami, the remains of the roast turkey, a glazed leg of ham, a side of smoked salmon, perhaps a bowl of cracked mud crabs, a basket of prawns cooked in olive oil and rosemary, a variety of cheeses and so on. Simple classic ingredients, ready on the table, at the disposal of the guests whenever they wish to eat. I must point out that this is not a cheap way of entertaining since it is essential that the quality be as fine as possible.

The wines are served in much the same way. Half a barrel full of cracked ice in which a couple of dozen bottles of white wine and champagne lie chilled. This may be repeated in another part of the house, by the dance floor for example. Any convenient sideboard can house a dozen reds and as long as there are plenty of glasses, guests soon get the idea.

This Open House Party is ideal at Christmas time and one may cater for over 100 people quite simply. I would suggest that this is also quite suitable for winter entertaining on much the same scale with perhaps the addition of a great steaming pot of soup which may be served in mugs. A huge cauldron of ham and pea soup, or a fish chowder.

Cooking and preparation time is not lengthy for this type of party, just roast the meat and cut the first few slices off each item to show the guests how the rest should be done. Let them help themselves and the host and hostess are left to enjoy themselves too!

COCKTAIL PARTY
Louis Ferguson

A Cocktail Party can be great fun and it is an ideal way to entertain a large group of friends. A cocktail is intended to stimulate the appetite, try not to overpower guests with drinks that are too potent and food that is too heavy. Make tiny canapés, the different combinations of flavours are limitless. A canapé is a platform or base of toast garnished and served as a savoury tit-bit, it can be picked up and eaten without utensils.

Hints for making cocktail canapés.
Watch the size when making canapés, a good savoury is only a mouthful. Do not be trapped into making them too ornate.
Depending on the Cocktail Party, allow between 4-8 canapés for each person. It is advisable to glaze the canapés with a savoury jelly, it improves the flavour and the appearance. One can buy packets of aspic jelly or prepare a mild chicken bouillon using chicken stock cubes and 1 oz of gelatine to every 1 pint of liquid.
Place a cocktail stick in each canapé so that your guests are able to pick them up with ease.
Cocktail canapés are best served on large trays with a centrepiece of fruit or garnished with crisp bunches of watercress or parsley.

Suitable foods for cocktail canapés.
Anchovy fillets, Asparagus spears, Beetroot, Blue Cheese, Capers, Caviare (red and black), Champignons, Cocktail onions, Cream cheese, Cucumber, Eggs, Frankfurters, Gherkins, Ham, Ham paste, Liverwurst, Mayonnaise, Mortadella sausage, Olives (black and stuffed), Pineapple, Prawns, Radishes, Red and green capsicums, Salami sausage, Salmon lax, Sardines, Seedless grapes, Shrimps, Smoked oysters, Sweet corn kernels, Walnuts.

Bases for Cocktail Canapés.
Although the bases or croûtes can be of toasted bread, fried bread, puff pastry, savoury biscuits or small choux pastry puffs, bread is by far the easiest base to prepare. There is a large variety of bread available and it can be cut into any small shape.

Preparation of Bread for Bases.
Toast bread on both sides and press under a weighted tray or board, or deep fry until golden brown and drain on absorbent paper. Another method for making canapé bases is to place bread on a buttered baking tray, brush the surface with melted butter and bake in a hot oven (400-450°F) until bread is crisp and brown. The bread may be toasted in slices or individual shapes. When using the second and third methods of preparation it is advisable to cut the bread into individual shapes before cooking. When making a large number of savouries, purchase an unsliced loaf of bread, remove the crust and slice lengthways.

Step by Step Preparation.
Prepare bases, calculating the quantity required by considering the particular occasion and the number of guests.
A 2 lb loaf of bread will make 100 canapé bases.
Prepare toppings and garnishes.
Prepare the savoury jelly and allow to cool.
Spread the bases lightly with butter.
Arrange toppings on the croûtes and place on wire cooling trays.
Refrigerate.
Place jelly over iced water and stir until of a syrupy consistency.
Coat each canapé with jelly and refrigerate until set.
Place on serving trays and garnish as desired.

Ideas for Cocktail Canapés.

● Cut buttered toast into rounds with a 1-inch cutter. Cover half of each croûte with red or black caviare, cover the other half with chopped hard-boiled egg white.

● Spread a slice of toast with softened cream cheese. Cover the entire surface with drained sweet corn kernels. Press well onto the cheese. Cut into diamond shapes and garnish with small diamonds of red capsicum.

● Cut buttered toast into rounds with a 1-inch cutter. Pipe a rosette of cream cheese on each croûte. Garnish with half a walnut or 3 seedless grapes.

● Cover a slice of buttered toast with ham. Cut into triangles and garnish with small pieces of pineapple.

● Cover a slice of buttered toast with well drained asparagus spears. Carefully cut into squares and garnish with a strip of red capsicum placed across each canapé diagonally.

● Cover a slice of buttered toast with salmon lax. Smooth surface with a knife and cut into diamonds. Garnish each with a scroll of butter.

● Cut buttered toast into rounds with a 1-inch cutter. Cut thin slices of salami the same size. Place onto croûtes and garnish with 3 peas held in place by a dab of French mustard.

● Place well drained sardines side by side down the length of a piece of toast. Cut toast into fingers between each fish. Garnish with small triangles of skinned lemon and sprinkle with a little cayenne pepper.

● Spread a slice of toast with liverwurst or liver paste. Cut into triangles with a knife dipped in hot water. Garnish with slices of black or stuffed olive.

● Spread a slice of buttered toast with creamed blue cheese. Cut into small rectangles with a knife dipped in hot water. Garnish with twists of sliced radish.

● Cut a slice of buttered toast into rounds with a 1-inch cutter. Place 2 shrimps around the outer edge to form a circle. Fill the centre with a little red or black caviare.

● Cut buttered toast into rounds with a 1-inch cutter. Pipe rosettes of sieved egg yolk blended with creamed butter and seasonings onto each croûte. Garnish with slices of gherkin.

● Cover a slice of buttered toast with drained anchovy fillets. Press down well and cut into diamonds. Garnish with pieces of smoked oyster.

● Cut buttered toast into rounds with a 1-inch cutter. Cut thin slices of beetroot the same size and place on croûtes. Garnish with halved cocktail onions.

● Cut buttered bread into small crescents. Cut crescents from slices of mortadella sausage and place them on croûtes. Garnish with 'zig zags' of creamed butter.

● Spread a slice of toast with creamed cheese. Cover with finely chopped red and green capsicum. Cut into diamonds with a wet knife.

● Spread a slice of toast with mustard butter. Cut into rectangles and cover with several thin slices of cooked frankfurter sausage.

● Cut buttered toast into small rectangles. Pipe a finger of creamed cheese down the length of each croûte. Garnish with slices of champignon.

DINNER PARTIES

Ted Moloney

There are no short cuts if a dinner party is to be successful. Good food means a certain amount of planning and work, even when a simple three course dinner is planned. Much of the preparation can be done at least a day or two in advance. This is the only way to manage, particularly if one is working 'single handed'. Having made a plan of work, the evening should flow smoothly and enjoyably from the moment your guests arrive.

Guide for a Successful Dinner Party.

Timing is important, be precise with your invitation. 'Come at seven o'clock, we shall sit down at a quarter to eight.' This should leave no doubt that reasonable promptness is expected.

The 'single handed' hostess can enterain up to six guests, eight in all, comfortably.

Serve dinner on time, even though your guests may be drinking cocktails happily, it is important they start to eat as well as drink!

Use place cards when seating six or more people. This is not pretentious, it is a sign of experience.

Plan your dinner menu so that you can prepare most of the food before the guests arrive. You can only manage last minute preparations for one course in a dinner menu. Guests should not be left sitting at the table for hours waiting for the next course to appear. Table marathons went out with the Edwardians!

Good conversation does help a dinner but the food should never suffer because of it.

Work to a plan set out in advance. Do this and you will avoid last minute chaos and confusion. Planning is essential when giving a dinner party of any kind.

48

formal dinner party

Planning a Successful Dinner Party.

I start by typing out two lists, the shopping list and the cooking schedule.

The Shopping List.

If it is to be a large party, write down the items to be bought on each of the days preceding the dinner party. Nothing is more tiring than coming home loaded with parcels and having to set to and cook all day long. Your kitchen is bound to get into a mess which will not help.

The only foods I buy on the day of the party are fish, vegetables and fruit, these must be fresh.

The meat can be bought two or three days in advance, beef especially.

Before making a shopping list, check with both butcher and greengrocer. Ask their advice about the best meat and vegetables available.

Cooking Schedule.

Having decided on the meat and vegetables, select your recipes. Many recipes may be partly cooked one or two days in advance and can be finished just before the guests arrive. This applies particularly to soups, sauces and fillings.

Write out a Cooking Schedule for—

A day or even two days before the party.

Cooking to be completed on morning of the party.

The cooking which must be left until the afternoon.

The last minute preparations. I even note down washing of lettuce and making of salad dressing. These jobs can be easily overlooked, so study each course carefully and decide how much can be prepared in advance.

Dinner Party Help.

Paid casual help has become very expensive and few people can afford to employ more than one person. Which should it be? A cook or a waiter? As you are a cook, a waiter is the answer, especially if you entertain often. Find the right man and use him always. Have him come early. He will be able to give glasses a last minute polish and set out the drinks for you. As he gets to know your ways you can leave him to keep an eye on things in the kitchen after you have sat down to dinner. Any party will run more smoothly when a man serves the drinks and waits at the table.

cocktail party

Host and Hostess.

Too many wives accept full responsibility for the dinner party. Give the man of the house his share of the spotlight. If your first course is soup, let him serve it from a tureen at the table. This gives the hostess an opportunity to get her breath back after the final preparations have been completed in the kitchen. The host may also serve the vegetables at the table if there is no waiter to pass them from guest to guest.

Give him a chafing dish and encourage him to take up table cooking, it is easy and fun. I have included a menu which is ideal for him to cook.

FORMAL DINNER PARTY

MENU
Oysters with Savoury
   Butter
Cauliflower Hollandaise
Duckling with Olives

New Potatoes
Lettuce and Watercress
   Salad
Crêpes Suzette

WINES
Chilled chablis

An auslese or spatlese white
   wine or a full flavoured
   red wine

Iced champagne or sauterne

Day Before:
Prepare Duckling with Olives and cook for 45 minutes.
Wash and dry lettuce and place in air-tight container in refrigerator.
Prepare watercress and place in a bowl of water in refrigerator.
Prepare French Dressing.
Make crêpes, place flat in an air-tight container with a round of waxed paper between each one, refrigerate.
Morning:
Prepare savoury butter for oysters.
Scrub new potatoes and place in a bowl of cold water.
Prepare cauliflower and place in a bowl of cold salted water.

50

Timetable:

5.30 p.m. Set table.
Assemble ingredients for Hollandaise Sauce and for finishing Duckling with Olives and Crêpes Suzette.
7.30 p.m. Place duckling in a moderate oven.
Spread oysters with savoury butter.
7.50 p.m. Grill oysters.
8.00 p.m. Boil potatoes.
Place Duckling with Olives on serving plate and garnish, cover carefully with foil and return to warm oven.
Serve oysters.
8.10 p.m. Make Hollandaise Sauce while changing plates and serve Cauliflower Hollandaise.
8.30 p.m. Drain potatoes, serve Duckling with Olives.
Toss sald in dressing.
Crêpes Suzette are cooked at the table.

OYSTERS WITH SAVOURY BUTTER

Temperature: 325–350°F

For each person allow:
2 oz butter
1 teaspoon Worcestershire sauce
1 clove garlic, crushed
1 shallot, finely chopped
1 tablespoon finely chopped parsley
8 oysters on the shell
fresh white breadcrumbs
paprika pepper

Cream butter with Worcestershire sauce, garlic, shallot and parsley. Spread each oyster with the savoury butter. Sprinkle with breadcrumbs. Place oysters on a wire rack on a baking tray. Lightly brown under a hot grill and place in a moderately slow oven to keep warm while remaining oysters are being browned under the grill. Sprinkle with a little paprika pepper and serve immediately.

CAULIFLOWER HOLLANDAISE

Serves: 8

1 cauliflower
½ pint Hollandaise Sauce
(see below)

sprigs of watercress or
parsley, for garnish

Choose a very young, white cauliflower, approximately 7-inches across. Trim stalk so that cauliflower will stand upright. Place 2 skewers through the stalk at right angles to each other and lower cauliflower gently, upside down, into a large saucepan of boiling, salted water. Boil until tender, 20-30 minutes, remove carefully, holding the skewers, drain. Keep cauliflower warm by standing in a colander over gently simmering water. Serve cauliflower coated with Hollandaise Sauce and garnish with sprigs of watercress or parsley.

HOLLANDAISE SAUCE

4 oz clarified butter
4 egg yolks

2 teaspoons lemon juice
salt and pepper

Place 1 oz of the clarified butter and 4 egg yolks in the top of a double boiler. Place over hot, but not boiling water, stir quickly and constantly with a wooden spoon until butter and eggs are well combined. Slowly add remaining butter, whisking the mixture constantly until sauce is well mixed and thickened. Remove top of double boiler from heat and beat sauce for 2 minutes. Add lemon juice, salt and pepper and place over hot water and beat for a further 2 minutes.
Note: Should the sauce curdle add 1-2 tablespoons of cold water and beat well until smooth.

DUCKLING WITH OLIVES

Time: 1½–2 hours
Temperature: 350–375°F
Serves: 8

2 x 3 lb ducklings
3 oz butter
1 tablespoon water
1 scant tablespoon (¼ oz) plain flour
1 cup dry white wine
½ cup fresh orange juice
½ cup tinned apricot juice

salt and pepper
6-inch piece of celery, 3 sprigs parsley, 1 bay leaf, 1 sprig of dried thyme, tied together
1 x 15 oz tin apricot halves
1 cup black olives

Remove fat from ducklings and truss. Heat 2 oz of the butter in a heavy based flameproof casserole and when sizzling, add ducklings and water. Cook birds over a moderate heat, uncovered, for 15 minutes on each side. Remove ducklings from casserole, pour off fat, leaving about 1 tablespoon of the pan juices in casserole. Place over heat and add remaining 1 oz butter. When melted, add flour and make a smooth roux. Stir until golden. Add warmed wine and fruit juices and stir until thickened. Season with salt and pepper. Add bunch of herbs and return ducklings to casserole. Cover casserole and place in a moderate oven for 1 hour or until ducklings are tender, one hour should be long enough if ducklings are really young. To serve, place ducklings on a heated serving plate and pour the pan juices over. Garnish with apricot halves and olives. Serve with boiled new potatoes.
Note: To make serving easier, the cooked ducklings may be cut into 4 portions in the kitchen before being garnished.

LETTUCE AND WATERCRESS SALAD

Serves: 8

1 large lettuce
1 bunch watercress
French Dressing
  (see below)

2 oz roquefort cheese

Wash and dry lettuce and tear into bite sized pieces, seal in plastic bag and place in refrigerator until ready to serve salad. Wash watercress and keep fresh by standing in a bowl of water in the refrigerator, break into neat sprigs when required. Mash roquefort cheese with a fork and add to French Dressing, combine thoroughly. To serve, place lettuce and watercress in a salad bowl, add the dressing and toss together.

FRENCH DRESSING

3 parts oil
1 part vinegar
½ teaspoon salt

½ teaspoon freshly ground
 pepper

Combine all ingredients in a screw-top jar and shake vigorously. Pour over salad just before serving and toss together until salad is coated with dressing.
Variations: Crushed garlic, French or English mustard or finely chopped herbs may be added to ingredients in jar.

CRÊPES SUZETTE

Serves: 8

Pancake batter:
½ cup (2 oz) plain flour
¾ teaspoon salt
4 eggs
1½ cups milk

3 oz butter
2 teaspoons grated lemon rind
clarified butter for cooking

For Crêpes Suzette:
1 tablespoon (1 oz) sugar
½ oz butter

1 tablespoon orange juice
1 tablespoon brandy
1 tablespoon grand marnier

Sift flour and salt into a bowl. Beat eggs and milk together. Make a well in the centre of the flour and gradually add liquid ingredients, beat until smooth. Add melted butter and lemon rind. Stand in refrigerator for 1 hour before using. Heat a heavy based 6-inch pancake pan and when hot, add a small piece of clarified butter, just enough to grease base of pan. Pour 1 tablespoon of the batter into pan. As batter hits hot surface of pan, lift and give a few quick twists and turns so batter spreads evenly. As soon as crêpe is 'bubbly' on upper surface, loosen edges with a palette knife and toss or turn crêpe. Do not allow the pan to get too hot. As the cooked pancakes are stacked, remove the pan from the heat for a few moments to help lose a little heat. Add only a minute amount of butter to pan in between making crêpes, just enough to keep pan greased.

To Complete Crêpes Suzette: Place sugar in chafing pan and place over a moderate flame until sugar starts to caramelise and melt. Stir and spread melting sugar so that it does not burn. Add butter and orange juice. Stir until well combined. Place the crêpes in the pan one at a time, folding them over twice so that they become quarters. When all are in the pan, simmer for 1 minute. Increase flame under pan, add brandy and grand marnier, count to 5 and ignite. Serve with a flourish!

Note: If chafing pan is not large enough to hold all the crêpes at the one time, heat in two stages.

CASSEROLE DINNER PARTY

This menu is ideal when the main course has to be prepared well in advance and reheated just before serving.

MENU
Salmon with Cucumber
   Sauce
Roulades
Boiled Rice
Tiny Peas and Onions
Viennese Baked Apples

WINES
Chilled moselle

Claret or burgundy

Night Before:
Make Roulades.
Shell peas and refrigerate.
Prepare filling for Viennese Baked Apples.

Timetable:
6.00 p.m. Chill salmon, peel and slice cucumbers and
marinate in dressing.
Set table.
7.00 p.m. Core and stuff apples.
Cook Tiny Peas and Onions.
7.30 p.m. Place Roulades in a moderate oven to heat.
Place rice in boiling salted water.
7.45 p.m. Place apples in oven to cook.
Drain rice, rinse well and place over
simmering water to keep warm.
Make cucumber sauce.
8.00 p.m. Serve dinner.
Drain peas and onions when changing plates
and increase oven temperature to hot for
apples.

SALMON WITH CUCUMBER SAUCE

Serves: 8

8 oz–1 lb. Canadian salmon	$\frac{1}{3}$ cup wine vinegar
2 cucumbers	salt and pepper
$\frac{2}{3}$ cup oil	$\frac{1}{4}$ pint sour cream

Chill salmon and place in the centre of a serving bowl.
Peel and thinly slice cucumbers. Mix oil and vinegar
together and pour over sliced cucumber. Sprinkle with
salt and pepper. Allow to stand for 1 hour, pressing
cucumber down into dressing frequently, drain.
Arrange half the cucumber slices around the salmon.
Just before serving, combine remaining cucumber with
sour cream and purée in an electric blender. Pour
cucumber sauce over salmon and serve immediately.

ROULADES

Time: 1½ hours
Temperature: 350–375°F
Serves: 8

1 x 3 lb piece fillet of beef
salt and pepper
seasoned flour
2 oz butter

Veal and pork filling:
8 oz mixed veal and pork,
  minced
1 tablespoon grated onion

Olive filling:
4 oz black olives

1 large ripe tomato
1½ cups red wine
1 x 5 oz tin tomato paste
¼ pint cream
1 tablespoon finely
  chopped parsley
salt and pepper

A 3 lb piece of fillet should make 2-3 Roulades per person.
Trim off all fat from fillet. Cut fillet into pieces approximately 3 × 4-inches and ¼-inch thick. Season with salt and pepper. Spread half the pieces of steak with veal and pork filling, roll up and tie neatly with white string or strong thread. Place black olives close together along centre of remaining pieces of steak, roll up and tie. Roll Roulades in seasoned flour. Melt butter in a heavy based flameproof casserole and when sizzling, brown Roulades all over. Remove from casserole, add tomato which has been skinned, seeded and chopped. Simmer for 1 minute and add wine. Bring to the boil, add tomato paste and stir until smooth. Stir in the cream, return Roulades to casserole. There should be enough liquid to just cover them. If there is not enough liquid, add a little more wine and cream. Cover casserole and simmer gently for 45 minutes. Reheat Roulades by placing in a moderate oven for 30 minutes. Serve with boiled rice.
Veal and Pork Filling: In a bowl, combine minced veal and pork, onion, parsley and salt and pepper. Beat together until ingredients are well combined.
Olive Filling: Wash brine off olives and remove stones.

58

TINY PEAS AND ONIONS

This is a recipe to keep in mind when you see very young peas and marble sized white onions at the greengrocer's shop.

Serves: 8

2 oz butter
8 tiny white onions
4 leaves of lettuce, shredded
1 scant tablespoon ($\frac{1}{2}$ oz) sugar
$\frac{1}{2}$ teaspoon salt
$\frac{1}{4}$ cup water
$1\frac{1}{2}$ lb young peas
extra $\frac{1}{2}$ oz butter
1 good tablespoon ($\frac{1}{2}$ oz) plain flour

Melt butter in a saucepan until sizzling. Add onions, lettuce, sugar, salt and water. Stir for a few seconds and add the peas. Bring to the boil, cover saucepan and simmer gently for 20 minutes, giving saucepan an occasional shake from time to time. Keep a little hot water handy, in case more liquid is required. By the time peas are tender, there should be no more than a few tablespoons of water in the bottom of the saucepan. Cream extra $\frac{1}{2}$ oz of butter together with flour until smooth. Stir and shake this into the peas over heat and as the small amount of liquid bubbles, the Tiny Peas and Onions are ready to serve.

VIENNESE BAKED APPLES

Time: 15–20 minutes
Temperature: 400–450°F
Serves: 8

8 Granny Smith apples
$\frac{1}{2}$ cup ground almonds
3 oz butter
1 tablespoon water
1 tablespoon honey
4 dried figs
1 cup dry breadcrumbs
$\frac{1}{2}$ cup (4 oz) sugar
$\frac{1}{2}$ pint cream, whipped, flavoured with curaçao

Core apples. Combine ground almonds, 1 oz of the melted butter, water and honey, mix together thoroughly. Cover base of a baking dish with aluminium foil and place cored apples in the dish. Halve the figs and push a piece into the centre of each apple, fill with honey and almond mixture. Pour remaining melted butter over apples. Combine breadcrumbs and sugar and sprinkle over apples. Bake in a hot oven for 15-20 minutes. Serve with whipped cream flavoured with curaçao.

THE MAN TAKES OVER

This is an easy dinner menu involving table cooking which any man can cope with successfully!

MENU
Smoked Ham with
  Rockmelon
Minute Steaks
Lyonnaise Potatoes
Green Salad
Cheese

WINES
Dry sherry

Claret or burgundy

Morning:
Boil potatoes in jackets for 20 minutes.
Prepare salad greens and refrigerate in an air-tight container.
Make French Dressing.

Timetable:
6.00 p.m. Beat steaks until $\frac{1}{4}$-inch thick.
             Assemble ingredients for Minute Steaks.
             Set table.
             Prepare Smoked Ham with Rockmelon and chill.
7.00 p.m. Prepare cheese board.
             Make Lyonnaise Potatoes, cover with aluminium foil and keep warm in a slow oven.
8.00 p.m. Serve dinner.
             Toss salad just before serving.

SMOKED HAM WITH ROCKMELON

Serves: 8

**1 lb Parma or prosciutto
ham, thinly sliced**   **2 ripe rockmelon**

Ask your delicatessen to slice the smoked ham
wafer thin. Peel, slice and seed the rockmelons just
before serving. Serve ham and prepared fruit on a
large platter or on individual serving plates.

MINUTE STEAKS

Time: 2–3 minutes
Serves: 8

8 pieces fillet steak, 1-inch thick

Steak champignon:
1 lb mushrooms, sliced

Steak Diane:
4 tablespoons finely chopped parsley

Paprika steak:
paprika pepper

salt and pepper
8 oz butter, for frying

½ pint cream

16 cloves garlic, crushed
8 teaspoons Worcestershire sauce

8 tablespoons brandy

Trim all fat off pieces of steak. Beat steaks with a meat mallet until a pancake size (approximately ¼-inch thick). Rub with salt and pepper. Place ingredients on a tray in the order in which they are to be used.
To cook minute steaks: Melt 1 oz of the butter in a chafing pan for each steak. When sizzling, add steak and fry for 1 minute on each side. Turn with tongs or a spoon and fork. Serve each steak as it is cooked and spoon over the pan juices. Ask guests to eat as soon as the Minute Steak is placed before them. Only a few minutes should elapse before the next steak is ready to serve.

Variations:
Steak champignon: Add some of the mushrooms to chafing pan at same time as steak. As steak is turned add 1 tablespoon cream for each steak. Lift out cooked steaks. Heat pan juices for 10 seconds over highest heat stirring continuously. Pour over steaks and serve.
Steak Diane: As steaks start to sizzle, sprinkle with chopped parsley and crushed garlic. As steak is turned, add 1 teaspoon of Worcestershire sauce, more garlic and parsley. Cook for 1 minute and serve.
Paprika steak: Sprinkle each side of steak generously with paprika pepper while cooking. Just before serving, add 1 tablespoon of brandy to pan for each steak, ignite and serve.

LYONNAISE POTATOES

Time: 20–30 minutes
Serves: 8

2 lb potatoes
8 oz onions
3 oz butter or margarine

salt and pepper
chopped parsley

Scrub potatoes and cook in boiling, salted water until almost tender. Peel and slice thinly. Peel onions, slice thinly and fry in butter in a frying pan until golden. Remove onion from pan and keep warm. Toss sliced potatoes in remaining butter in pan until golden brown and fat has been absorbed, add onion and season to taste with salt and pepper. Sprinkle with chopped parsley before serving.

GREEN SALAD

Serves: 8

1 large lettuce
1 green capsicum
1 cup celery, sliced

French Dressing (see page 54)

Wash and dry lettuce, tear into bite sized pieces. Remove seeds from capsicum and cut into thin strips. Place lettuce, capsicum and celery in salad bowl, cover and chill. When ready to serve, add French Dressing and toss salad gently and thoroughly.

BUFFET DINNER PARTIES

Gretta Anna Teplitzky

Buffet dinner parties are an ideal way to entertain a large number of guests. Australians are well known for the success and enjoyment of these occasions. They have become almost a way of life, friendly, relaxed, informal gatherings where the guests may circulate freely. The

The success of a party does not depend upon the amount of money spent on lavish food and drink, but it does require a host and hostess who really enjoy entertaining, who are interested in their guests and are sufficiently well organized so that they can relax with their friends and enjoy themselves. The art of entertaining, like all other arts, needs plenty of practise and an ability to organize the preparations in advace. Hostesses today have the added pleasure and convenience of efficient equipment for preparation, cooking and storage of their party menus, so that they can cope with a large buffet dinner party 'single handed'. Planning ahead however is still very necessary for the party's success. If a menu is chosen which can be prepared in advance, everything will run smoothly and the hostess will be able to enjoy her party along with her guests. Buffet parties are particularly suitable for weddings, birthdays and anniversary celebrations, where a large number of people can be easily entertained.

64

summer buffet dinner party

Guides for successful Buffet Dinner Parties.

Choose food that is easy to serve and that can be eaten standing up with only a fork. Meat, vegetables and salads should be cut into bite sized pieces and appetizers and desserts should be served in small, easily handled portions, which can be eaten with a fork, a spoon or in the fingers.

Choose dishes which can be prepared before the party, leaving only the finishing touches to be completed just before serving.

Offer a variety of dishes when catering for a large number of people. The food should be displayed on a long table, bearing in mind that a number of people will be serving themselves at the same time. Arrange plates, forks and napkins at convenient places on the table and encourage guests to help themselves.

Serve a choice of red and white wine and serve drinks from a separate improvised 'bar'. Place small tables and chairs in convenient places so that older guests may sit down.

SUMMER BUFFET DINNER PARTY

MENU
Rare Roast Beef with
   Cumquats
Cold Roast Chicken and
   Lemon Mustard
   Mayonnaise
Lima Bean and Cauliflower
   Salad
Sour Cream and Caraway
   Coleslaw
Spinach and Watercress
   Salad
Champignons and
   Artichoke Salad
Peaches Italienne
Coffee

open house party

Two Days Before:
Prepare and marinate mushrooms.
Day Before:
Cook fillets of beef and chickens, wrap in aluminium foil, seal tightly and place in refrigerator.
Cook lima beans and cauliflower flowerettes, drain, cool, cover with clear plastic or aluminium foil and refrigerate.
Chop vegetables and herbs for Lima Bean and Cauliflower Salad, wrap separately and refrigerate. Make Sour Cream and Caraway Coleslaw, store covered in refrigerator.
Wash and dry lettuce, spinach and watercress. Store lettuce and spinach in an air-tight container in refrigerator. Place watercress in water in refrigerator.
Hard-boil eggs.
Prepare salad dressings.
Morning:
Remove chicken flesh from bones and cut into bite sized pieces. Make lemon mustard mayonnaise, chill in refrigerator.
Assemble ingredients for Champignons and Artichoke Salad.
Prepare peaches, fill with macaroon filling and refrigerate.

Timetable:
5.30 p.m. Set buffet table.
Pour sherry over peaches and heat in oven.
6.00 p.m. Fold chicken pieces into lemon mustard mayonnaise, arrange on serving plate and garnish.
Carve beef, garnish with cumquats.
Combine ingredients for Lima Bean and Cauliflower Salad and Champignons and Artichoke Salad, pour dressings over and toss.
7.30 p.m. Guests arrive.
7.50 p.m. Whip cream.
Toss Spinach and Watercress Salad.
8.00 p.m. Serve buffet dinner.

66

RARE ROAST BEEF WITH CUMQUATS

Although the fillet is an expensive piece of beef, it cuts into many thin slices and there is no waste.

Time: 1¼ hours
Temperature: 350–375°F
Serves: 20

2 x 3 lb eye or Scotch
   fillets of beef
salt and pepper

2 cups oil
fresh cumquats and sprigs
   of mint, for garnish

Ask the butcher to select short, chunky fillets rather than long, thin ones. Trim the fillets of any large pieces of fat, season with salt and pepper and place in a roasting pan. Pour the oil over and roast in a moderate oven for approximately 1¼ hours, basting several times while cooking. Remove the fillets and place on pieces of aluminium foil, cool and spoon 7-8 tablespoons of juice from the pan onto them. Wrap and seal tightly in the foil and place in the refrigerator until required. Serve thinly sliced, garnished with peeled cumquats and sprigs of mint.

Note: Any meat to be served cold can be cooked the day before as long as it is stored in aluminium foil, in the refrigerator, and is moistened well with juice from the pan.

COLD ROAST CHICKEN WITH LEMON MUSTARD MAYONNAISE

Time: **2 hours**
Temperature: **325–350°F**
Serves: **20**

4 x 3 lb chickens
salt and pepper
2 cups oil

For lemon mustard
   mayonnaise:
5 egg yolks
3 teaspoons grated lemon
   rind
3 teaspoons prepared
   English mustard
3 teaspoons sugar

Marinated Mushrooms, for
   garnish (see page 69)

1 teaspoon salt
2 teaspoons crumbled dried
   tarragon
1 teaspoon paprika pepper
3 cups salad oil
$4\frac{1}{2}$ tablespoons lemon
   juice
3 tablespoons vinegar

Clean chickens, removing the neck and innards, sprinkle with salt and pepper and place in a roasting pan. Pour the oil over the chickens and roast in a moderately slow oven turning and basting several times, for approximately 2 hours or until tender. Place the chickens on pieces of aluminium foil, spoon 8-12 tablespoons of juice from the pan onto them. Wrap and seal the foil tightly around the chickens while still warm and place in the refrigerator until required.
Carefully remove the chicken from the bones, cut into bite sized pieces, discarding the skin. Fold the chicken pieces into some of the lemon mustard mayonnaise and pile in the centre of a large platter. Surround the chicken with salad greens and garnish with Marinated Mushrooms. Serve the remaining mayonnaise separately in a bowl.

To make lemon mustard mayonnaise: Beat the egg yolks until they are thick. Add the lemon rind, English mustard, sugar, salt, tarragon, and paprika pepper and mix well. Beat in the salad oil, a spoonful at a time, beating continuously. When well mixed, gradually add the lemon juice and the vinegar. Chill and serve with the chicken.

Note: The chickens may be cooked the day before as long as they are stored in aluminium foil in the refrigerator and are well basted with chicken juice from the pan. Cheaper frozen chickens respond well to this method.

MARINATED MUSHROOMS

1½ lb button mushrooms
2 tablespoons chopped
  chives
2 tablespoons chopped
  shallots
1½ cups oil

½ cup white wine vinegar
salt and pepper
2 teaspoons French
  mustard
1 teaspoon paprika pepper

The mushrooms need not be washed or peeled. Wipe lightly with a damp cloth. Place all ingredients in a mixing bowl or a large jar and toss occasionally. Leave from 6-48 hours. To serve, drain mushrooms well and use to garnish platters of cold meat.

LIMA BEAN AND CAULIFLOWER SALAD

Serves: 20

8 oz lima beans
½ cauliflower
2 tablespoons chopped chives
2 tablespoons chopped shallots

For dressing:
6 tablespoons oil
2 tablespoons vinegar
salt and pepper

1 red capsicum, chopped
1 tablespoon chopped mint
1 tablespoon chopped parsley
2 cloves garlic, crushed
3 teaspoons dried basil

1 teaspoon French mustard
1 teaspoon paprika pepper

Cook lima beans until tender in boiling, salted water, approximately 1½ hours. Do not soak overnight as this tends to make the beans lose their skins. Drain and cool. Break the cauliflower into flowerettes and parboil for 5 minutes, drain and cool. Combine beans, cauliflower and remaining ingredients.
To make dressing: Shake all the ingredients together in a screw-top jar. Pour dressing over the salad, toss and serve chilled.
Note: This salad may be made several hours before serving. If you wish to do most of the work the day before, prepare everything and combine ingredients an hour or so before serving.

SOUR CREAM AND CARAWAY COLESLAW

Serves: 20

½ large cabbage
4 tablespoons tarragon
  vinegar
salt and pepper
1 green capsicum
2 teaspoons celery seeds

1 teaspoon caraway seeds
3 tablespoons Mayonnaise
  (see page 72)
3 tablespoons sour cream
1 teaspoon paprika pepper

Shred the cabbage finely and add the vinegar and salt
and pepper. Chop the capsicum finely. Add chopped
capsicum, celery and caraway seeds to cabbage and
mix. Lastly add the Mayonnaise and sour cream. Toss
together thoroughly and chill. Serve sprinkled with
paprika pepper.
Note: This salad may be completed several hours or
even the day before serving.

MAYONNAISE

Home-made Mayonnaise is so much better than any commercial variety. It is worthwhile making your own as it will keep very well in the refrigerator for over a fortnight.

1–2 egg yolks
1 teaspoon white wine
  vinegar
½ teaspoon salt

½ teaspoon dry mustard
pinch of white pepper
¼ pint olive oil
few drops of lemon juice

Make sure your mixing bowl is well washed and dried. In it beat egg yolks, vinegar, salt, dry mustard and pepper with a rotary beater. Add olive oil, drop by drop, whisking continuously, until about 2 tablespoons have been added. Add a few drops of lemon juice, to bring to the consistency of cream. Add the remaining oil in a thin steady stream, beating continuously, stopping the addition of the oil from time to time to make sure the mixture is combining well. When all the oil has been added and the Mayonnaise is thick, add extra lemon juice to taste. Adjust seasoning. The Mayonnaise when completed should be stiff enough to support its own trail. Use as required.

Note: Should the mixture curdle, wash the beater, beat 1 egg yolk in another bowl and very slowly add the curdled Mayonnaise to the fresh egg yolk, beating continuously. If an electric beater is used set it at medium speed.

SPINACH AND WATERCRESS SALAD

Serves: 20

1 small lettuce
½ bunch young spinach
3 bunches watercress
  sprigs
1½ tablespoons pine nuts or
  pumpkin seeds (peppitas)
1½ tablespoons sunflower
  seed kernels

pinch of nutmeg
1 teaspoon grated lemon
  rind
salt and pepper
4–5 tablespoons oil
1½–2 tablespoons vinegar

Wash lettuce and spinach, shake off excess water and pat dry in a clean tea towel and store in an air-tight container in the refrigerator until serving time. Keep the watercress under water in a basin in the refrigerator. Have all the other ingredients ready and at serving time tear the lettuce and spinach into a salad bowl, shake the watercress free of water and add, then add all other ingredients, toss well and serve.
Note: Pine nuts, pumpkin seeds and sunflower seed kernels are obtainable at health food stores.

CHAMPIGNONS AND ARTICHOKE SALAD

Serves: 20

1 x 15 oz tin artichoke
   hearts, well drained
1 x 15 oz tin champignons
4 hard-boiled eggs
2 tablespoons chopped
   sweet gherkins

1 lb prawns, peeled
1 tablespoon chopped
   shallots

For dressing:
½ cup oil
1½ tablespoons vinegar

salt and pepper
1 teaspoon French mustard

Cut the artichoke hearts in halves and place in a salad
bowl. Add the drained champignons, hard-boiled
eggs cut into quarters, gherkins, prawns and shallots.
To make dressing: Shake all ingredients together in a
screw-top jar. When ready to serve salad, pour dressing
over and mix carefully.
Note: The ingredients for this salad may be prepared
the day before and the salad can then be completed
several hours before serving.

PEACHES ITALIENNE

Time: 7–10 minutes
Temperature: 350–375°F
Serves: 20

5 x 30 oz tins peach halves
or 20–24 fresh peaches
poached in syrup, stoned
and halved

For macaroon filling:
40 almond macaroons
5 tablespoons mixed grated
orange and lemon rind

$4\frac{1}{2}$ cups sweet sherry
whipped cream, for serving

$3\frac{1}{2}$ tablespoons lemon juice

Drain the peach halves and place them in large shallow
ovenproof dishes, spoon macaroon filling into the
cavity of each. Pour the sherry over the peaches and
heat in a moderate oven for approximately 7-10 minutes.
Serve hot or cold, spooning some of the sherry onto
each. Serve with whipped cream.
To make macaroon filling: Crumble macaroons and
mix with orange and lemon rind and lemon juice.

WINTER BUFFET DINNER PARTY

MENU
Prawns in Garlic and
  Anchovy Sauce
Party Boeuf à la Bourguig-
  nonne
Chicken with Sherry
Scandinavian Potatoes
Toasted Almond and Fennel
  Green Salad
Fraises dans la Neige
Coffee

Day Before:
Prepare and cook Party Boeuf à la Bourguignonne
until tender. Cool, cover and refrigerate.
Roast chicken, cool, cut into portions, cover securely
and refrigerate.
Wash and dry lettuce and aniseed, place in an air-tight
container and refrigerate.
Toast and chop almonds for salad.
Chop shallots and parsley for salad and garnish, wrap
separately and refrigerate.
Make French Dressing.

Morning:
Make Fraises dans la Neige and refrigerate.
Prepare Scandinavian Potatoes and bake for 1 hour.
Complete Chicken with Sherry, cook for 1 hour, cool.
Boil onions and sauté mushrooms for Party Boeuf à la
Bourguignonne.
Peel prawns and assemble ingredients for Prawns in
Garlic and Anchovy Sauce and for Scandinavian
Potatoes.

Timetable:

5.30 p.m. Set buffet table.
7.00 p.m. Place potatoes in a moderate oven.
7.30 p.m. Guests arrive.
Place Party Boeuf à la Bourguignonne and
Chicken in Sherry in the oven to heat.
Re-mix Fraises dans la Neige gently and
spoon into individual serving glasses.
7.45 p.m. Cook Prawns in Garlic and Anchovy Sauce.
8.00 p.m. Toss salad.
Serve buffet dinner.

PRAWNS IN GARLIC AND ANCHOVY SAUCE

Time: 10–15 minutes
Serves: 20

4½ lb prawns
1 lb butter
2 x 1¾ oz tins anchovy
   fillets

4 cloves garlic, crushed
2 sticks French bread

Peel prawns. Place in a large pan with melted butter,
mashed anchovies and garlic. Heat and mix
thoroughly. Serve hot in individual ramekins with
crisp French bread, unbuttered, cut into slices or cubes.

PARTY BOEUF À LA BOURGUIGNONNE

Time: 2–2½ hours
Serves: 20

6 lb stewing beef
3 good tablespoons (1½ oz)
  plain flour
3 tablespoons oil
1½ lb salt pork
8 rashers bacon, chopped
4 carrots, chopped
8 shallots, chopped
2 onions, chopped
2 cloves garlic, crushed
extra 3 tablespoons oil
2 stalks celery, chopped
2 bay leaves
salt and pepper

8 pieces bone cut just
  above calf's foot
  (optional)
5 cups burgundy
3½ cups beef stock or water
  and beef stock cubes
1 cup brandy
2 tablespoons chopped
  parsley
36 small onions, boiled
36 small mushrooms,
  sautéed
chopped parsley, for
  garnish

Trim the beef and cut into large cubes, dip in flour and sauté in 3 tablespoons oil until golden, together with the salt pork, cut in cubes and the bacon. Transfer all meat to a large saucepan. Sauté the carrots, shallots, onions and garlic in the extra oil until golden and add to the saucepan. Add celery, bay leaves, salt and pepper and the bones. Simmer the burgundy in a small saucepan until it is reduced to half its original quantity and add to the beef and vegetables together with the beef stock, brandy and chopped parsley. Bring to the boil, reduce heat and simmer gently, covered, until the meat is tender, approximately 2-2½ hours. Remove the bones and add the cooked onions and mushrooms. Reheat and serve sprinkled with chopped parsley.

CHICKEN WITH SHERRY

Time: 1¾–2 hours
Temperature: 350–375°F
Serves: 20

3 x 3 lb chickens
6 tablespoons oil
3 good tablespoons (1½ oz)
   plain flour
salt and pepper
7 oz butter
7 tablespoons oil
1–1½ lb mushrooms, sliced

½ pint cream
¼ pint milk
1½ cups dry sherry
¾ cup chicken stock or
   water and chicken stock
   cube
chopped parsley, for
   garnish

Roast the chickens, smeared with 6 tablespoons oil, in
a moderate oven for 30 minutes, cool and cut into
serving portions. Dip the chicken pieces in the flour,
sprinkle with salt and pepper and sauté until golden
in the butter and oil. Place the chicken in an ovenproof
casserole. Sauté the mushrooms in the remaining
butter and oil for 5-7 minutes and add to the chicken.
Pour the cream, milk and sherry into the pan and
simmer for 10 minutes, stirring in all the browning
from the bottom of the pan and pour over chicken.
Add chicken stock. Cover and cook in a moderate
oven for approximately 1¼ hours or until the chicken
is tender. Serve sprinkled with chopped parsley.

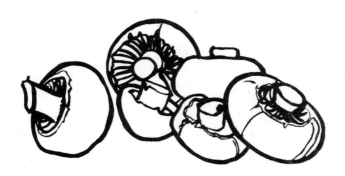

SCANDINAVIAN POTATOES

Time: $1\frac{1}{2}$–2 hours
Temperature: 350–375°F
Serves: 20

6 onions, sliced $1\frac{1}{2}$–2 cups grated cheese
2 oz butter   salt and pepper
3 tablespoons oil   4 oz butter
14 large potatoes $\frac{3}{4}$ pint cream

Sauté the onions in the butter and oil until soft. Place
in a buttered ovenproof casserole alternating with
layers of thinly sliced potato and grated cheese.
Arrange 3 layers of each, starting and finishing with
potato and adding salt and pepper to each layer of
potato. Dot with the butter and pour the cream into
the casserole. Bake uncovered in a moderate oven for
approximately $1\frac{1}{2}$-2 hours.

the man takes over

TOASTED ALMOND AND FENNEL GREEN SALAD

Serves: 20

3 lettuce
4 oz almonds, blanched and
toasted
½ root aniseed

For French dressing:
1 cup oil
⅓ cup vinegar

pinch of fennel (optional)
8 shallots, chopped
2 tablespoons chopped
parsley

2 teaspoons French
mustard
salt and pepper

Wash lettuce, shake off excess water and pat dry with
a clean tea towel, place in an air-tight container in the
refrigerator until serving time. Chop the almonds.
Wash the aniseed and slice thinly.
To make French Dressing: Place all the ingredients in a
screw-top jar and shake well.
When ready to serve the salad, tear the lettuce into a
salad bowl, add the other ingredients, shake the
dressing in the jar and pour over the salad, toss and
serve.

after theatre party

FRAISES DANS LA NEIGE

Serves: 20

4–5 boxes strawberries
icing sugar to taste
9 egg whites
15 oz icing sugar
1 cup brandy

3 heaped teaspoons grated
   orange rind
4½ teaspoons rose water
1½ pints cream

Slice the strawberries (retain a few for decoration) and
sprinkle with a little icing sugar to taste, stand for
15 minutes. Whisk the egg whites until stiff and
gradually beat in the 15 oz icing sugar, beating all the
time. Add the brandy, grated orange rind and rose
water. Whip the cream and fold in gently. Add the
strawberries and mix in gently. Allow to stand in the
refrigerator for several hours. Just before serving,
re-mix gently (as some brandy may have separated out)
and spoon into individual serving glasses.
Note: Rose water is obtainable from any leading
chemist.

AFTER THEATRE PARTY

Oscar Mendelsohn

Having a dinner party before going to the theatre is not always satisfactory. The thought of being held up by traffic on the way to the theatre, arriving late for some reason or other does not make for a relaxing atmosphere. Have a snack before leaving home and ask friends to join you afterwards for something tasty to eat and a nightcap. Make sure the food served is full of flavour but not overpowering. Either serve a selection of the following delicious, savoury dishes or make one or two of them in larger quantities.

Serve Cheesed Onions piping hot, Scotch Woodcock on hot buttered toast, Welsh Rarebit or creamy Scrambled Eggs and Tomatoes (see page 10). The number of dishes suitable for an After Theatre Party is innumerable. All these dishes are easy to prepare when you arrive home or can be prepared to a certain stage beforehand, adding the final touches on arriving home.

Serve red wine or chilled white wine. Later serve freshly percolated coffee. What a relaxing way to end a pleasant evening.

ANGELS ON HORSEBACK

Time: 5–6 minutes
Temperature: 400–450 °F
Serves: 4

8 large fresh oysters   pepper
4 thin rashers lean bacon or paprika pepper (optional)
  smoked ham

Open, drain and remove oysters from shells. Remove
rind from bacon. Cut rashers in half. Wrap each oyster
in a piece of bacon or smoked ham and place on a skewer.
Sprinkle with pepper and, if desired, paprika pepper.
Cook under a hot grill or place on a baking tray and
cook in a hot oven for 5-6 minutes or until bacon is
crisp.

CHEESED ONIONS

Time: **35 minutes**
Temperature: **350–375°F**
Serves: **4**

6 large white onions
4 slices buttered toast
4 oz mature cheese, grated
2 eggs

$\frac{1}{2}$ pint milk
$\frac{1}{2}$ teaspoon salt
$\frac{1}{4}$ teaspoon curry powder
1 oz butter

Peel and slice the oions, boil until tender and drain thoroughly. Place slices of buttered toast in a shallow ovenproof casserole. Spread a layer of onion on the toast and cover with cheese. Beat eggs and milk together thoroughly, add salt and curry powder, pour over the onions and cheese and dot with butter. Bake in a moderate oven for approximately 35 minutes. Serve piping hot.

DEVILLED POULTRY WINGS

Time: 15–25 minutes
Serves: 4

2 oz butter
4 poultry wings
$\frac{1}{2}$ cup dry breadcrumbs
2 tablespoons wine vinegar
1 clove garlic
1 teaspoon dry mustard
$\frac{1}{2}$ teaspoon salt

$\frac{1}{4}$ teaspoon pepper
pinch of cayenne pepper
extra 1 oz butter
1 teaspoon Worcestershire
   sauce
1 teaspoon soya sauce

Melt butter in frying pan. Add cooked or raw poultry
wings. When golden brown, remove from pan and roll
in breadcrumbs until thickly coated. Return to the
pan, adding a little more butter if required, cook until
the coating is crisp and chicken is tender. Place wings
on a hot plate and keep warm. Add vinegar, garlic,
dry mustard, salt, pepper and a pinch of cayenne
pepper to remaining butter in pan and heat until
contents are reduced by half. Remove the garlic and
add the extra butter, Worcestershire sauce and soya
sauce. Mix well. Pour sauce over the wings and
serve immediately.
Note: Other portions of poultry may be substituted for
wings. Large wings or legs may be halved with poultry
shears before cooking.

FANDANGO SARDINES

Time: 5 minutes
Temperature: 300–325 °F
Serves: 4

1 x 4⅜ oz tin sardines
2 slices bread
1 tablespoon anchovy
   paste
Lemon butter:
2 oz butter

1 tablespoon finely
   chopped parsley

1 tablespoon lemon juice
pinch of cayenne pepper

Drain sardines and place in a frying pan and heat gently, turning once. Remove crusts from bread and cut into fingers, toast and spread with anchovy paste that has been mixed with the parsley. Place 1 sardine on each piece of toast and reheat for 5 minutes in a slow oven. Place a small piece of lemon butter on top of each sardine before serving.
To make lemon butter: Cream butter until soft. Gradually beat in lemon juice and cayenne pepper.
Note: Use large Spanish sardines in this recipe.

OSBORNE OYSTERS

Time: 2–3 minutes
Serves: 4

8 large fresh oysters   1 oz Swiss cheese, grated
1 ripe banana   1 teaspoon lemon juice

Open and drain oysters, leaving them on the half shell.
Place a round slice (approximately $\frac{1}{4}$-inch thick) of
banana on each oyster. Sprinkle with cheese and lemon
juice and place under a hot grill until cheese bubbles.
Avoid overcooking as oysters will toughen. Serve
immediately.

SALAMI CUPS

Time: 5 minutes
Serves: 4

6 oz salami sausage, in the piece

filling as desired
finely chopped parsley

Cut salami into approximately 20 slices without removing the skin. (This is important as it is the restraining force of the skin that shapes the flat sausage into a cup). Place under a hot grill until the cups are formed. Remove and drain on absorbent paper. Peel off the skin and partly fill each cup with a small amount of mango chutney, French mustard, ketchup, grated cheese or crushed pineapple. Sprinkle with parsley and place under the grill until heated. Serve immediately.

SATANIC SARDINES

Time: 2 minutes
Serves: 4

1 x 4⅜ oz tin sardines
2 slices brown bread
1 oz butter
pinch of pepper
½ teaspoon curry powder

1 teaspoon lemon juice
1 teaspoon finely chopped
  parsley
½ teaspoon finely chopped
  onion

Drain sardines. Toast the bread on both sides, remove the crusts and spread with butter. Cut each slice in half. Place a sardine on each and sprinkle with pepper, curry powder and lemon juice. Place under a hot grill for 1-2 minutes. Sprinkle with parsley and onion and serve immediately.
Note: Use large Spanish sardines in this recipe.

SCOTCH WOODCOCK

Time: 10 minutes
Serves: 4

1 x 1¾ oz tin anchovy fillets
2 slices bread
2 oz butter
2 eggs

1 tablespoon milk
cayenne pepper
salt

Drain anchovy fillets. Toast bread, remove the crusts and spread with half the butter. Beat eggs with milk, adding cayenne pepper and salt to taste. Melt remaining butter in a saucepan, add the egg mixture and cook over a gentle heat, stirring continuously. When thickened to desired consistency, place on the toast and arrange thin fillets of anchovy on top. Cut each slice into 4 fingers. Place briefly under a hot grill and serve immediately.

SMOKED SALMON HORNS

Serves: 4

2 oz smoked salmon
1 oz caviare
freshly ground black
 pepper

1 teaspoon lemon juice
slices of orange, for garnish

Cut thin slices of smoked salmon into triangular shapes. Roll each into the shape of a horn or cone, fill with caviare and secure with a cocktail stick. Sprinkle with black pepper and lemon juice. Arrange on a serving plate and garnish with slices of orange. Chill before serving.

WELSH RAREBIT

Time: 10 minutes
Serves: 4

2 oz butter
½ pint beer
8 oz mature Cheddar
 cheese, grated
½ teaspoon salt
¼ teaspoon dry mustard

pinch of paprika pepper
 (optional)
½ teaspoon Worcestershire
 sauce (optional)
2 thin slices white bread

Melt butter in the top of a double saucepan and stir in the warmed beer. Add cheese gradually, stirring with a wooden spoon until melted and smooth. Add salt, mustard, paprika pepper and Worcestershire sauce. Cut sliced bread diagonally into two and toast. Spread with cheese mixture and place under a hot grill until bubbling. Serve immediately.

Variation: If preferred, use large water biscuits in place of the toast. Heat biscuits before spreading with the cheese mixture.

PATIO
PARTY

Daphne Eilers

A Patio Party must be carefully planned with food and drinks prepared in advance so that when the guests arrive the host and hostess are able to introduce their friends to one another. Plan the menu ahead and make out a programme of work. This will help you to relax on the day, knowing everything is organised and that you will only have to garnish dishes and toss salads before serving the meal. Colour is important, try to use bright cloths, serviettes and your gayest serving dishes and china. The presentation of the food is important. Guests will serve themselves and the whole setting should be pleasing to the eye. Food will be eaten with the fingers or with a fork, so choose suitable dishes. Offer a variety of courses and include some hot dishes, particularly for an evening party. Hot dishes may stand on food warmers.

Due to our wonderful climatic conditions, many houses have a patio—a paved area outside the house, where families and friends may gather and have meals out of doors in the fresh air. Patios are often close to a pool where guests may swim when they arrive. It is a help if it is close to the kitchen so that food may be prepared and carried outdoors easily. Suitable lighting and furniture is important. The lighting should be effective but not too bright. Furniture must be sturdy so that it may remain outside when not in use. It is a good idea to have an area protected by a pergola or where a beach umbrella may be put up. The food may then be arranged on tables in the shade.

94

Collect this type of equipment gradually and you will be amazed at the different effects you will be able to achieve with each table setting. Decorate the table, use candles and flowers or anything else which will help you achieve the right atmosphere. Serve cold drinks in tall glasses with plenty of ice, or hot soups in sturdy pottery mugs.

All age groups, particularly teenagers, will enjoy a Patio Party if it is well organised and there is a gay atmosphere. It is the ideal setting for meeting people, put on your favourite records and have fun with your friends!

PATIO PARTY
Avocado Appetizer
Seafood Risotto
Pork Kebabs
Chicken Italian Style
Greek Marrow Salad
Piquant Salad
Apricot Whip
Coffee

Two Days Before:
Prepare Fish Stock.
One Day Before:
Cook rice in Fish Stock.
Make barbecue sauce.
Cook chicken, cool, cut meat into cubes.
Make sauce for Chicken Italian Style, cover with wet, greaseproof paper and refrigerate.
Make salad dressings.
Morning:
Prepare kebabs and refrigerate.
Prepare Greek Marrow Salad.
Prepare Piquant Salad, but do not add apple.
Make Apricot Whip.
Peel and segment grapefruit, cover and refrigerate.
Complete Chicken Italian Style.

Timetable:
6.00 p.m. Set table.
7.00 p.m. Place Chicken Italian Style in a moderate oven until ready to serve dinner.
Prepare Avocado Appetizer.
7.30 p.m. Cook crayfish and complete Seafood Risotto.
Add diced apple to Piquant Salad.
8.00 p.m. Serve dinner.

AVOCADO APPETIZER

Serves: 10

5 avocado pears   **8 oz cottage cheese**
5 grapefruit

Wipe avocado pears and then cut in halves lengthways.
Remove stones. Carefully cut out the flesh making
sure the skins are left intact. Cube the flesh. Peel the
grapefruit with a sharp knife removing pith and
membrane so that grapefruit sections can be removed
whole. Cut each section of grapefruit in half. Pile the
mixture of grapefruit and avocado back into the half
avocado skins and top with a spoonful of cottage cheese.
Chill before serving.

Variation: If preferred, yoghurt may replace the cheese.

patio party

SEAFOOD RISOTTO

Time: 45 minutes
Serves: 10

1 cup olive oil
2 onions, thinly sliced
1½ lb rice
3 pints Fish Stock (see
   page 98)

1 large crayfish
4 oz tasty cheese, grated
salt and pepper
24 mussels or cockles

Heat ¾ cup oil in a deep saucepan, add the onions and
sauté until soft and clear yellow. Stir in the rice and
cook until well coated with oil and slightly coloured.
Add some of the hot Fish Stock and cook gently until
liquid is absorbed, add more stock as needed. Stir
frequently to prevent sticking. The rice should cook in
20 minutes. Remove crayfish from shell and cut into
cubes and warm in remaining heated oil. When rice
is soft, add the warmed crayfish and the grated cheese.
Adjust seasoning to taste. Pile risotto onto a serving
dish and garnish with the crayfish legs and opened
mussels.

To prepare mussels: Wash well and using only unopened
ones, place in a steamer above boiling water. Steam,
covered, for 5-10 minutes until they open. Remove
beards from mussels before placing on dish of risotto.

barbecue

FISH STOCK

1½ lb fish bones or
  trimmings
1 tomato, chopped
2 sprigs parsley
1 bay leaf

1 large onion, sliced
1 clove garlic, crushed
2 teaspoons salt
6 peppercorns
3½ pints cold water

Wash fish bones or trimmings well. Place in a large saucepan with other ingredients. Cover saucepan and bring to the boil. Reduce heat and simmer for 1 hour. Strain before using.

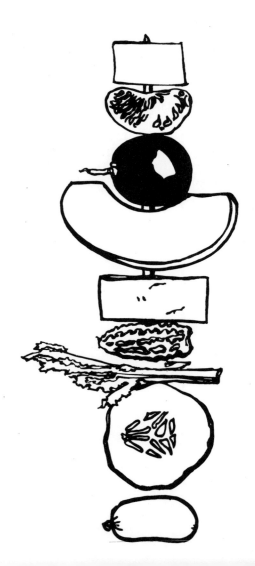

PORK KEBABS

Time: 30–40 minutes
Temperature: 350–375°F
Serves: 10

$2\frac{1}{2}$ lb pork fillets
5 onions
8 oz lean bacon
20 mushrooms, wiped and
    destalked

For barbecue sauce:
$\frac{1}{2}$ cup tomato purée
2 tablespoons vinegar
$\frac{1}{4}$ cup soy sauce
1 teaspoon French mustard

1 x 15 oz tin pineapple
    pieces

2 good tablespoons (1 oz)
    brown sugar
2 teaspoons grated green
    ginger
2 cloves garlic, crushed

Cut the pork fillets into $\frac{3}{4}$-inch slices. Slice the onions into $\frac{1}{2}$-inch slices. Cut the bacon into bite sized pieces. Thread a mushroom onto each skewer, alternate pieces of pork, pineapple, onion and bacon along the length of the skewer. Finish with a second mushroom. Brush liberally with barbecue sauce and either grill slowly over hot charcoal for 30-35 minutes or bake in a moderate oven for 30-40 minutes. While cooking, turn the skewers and brush again with the barbecue sauce. Serve hot with any remaining barbecue sauce. To make Barbecue Sauce: Mix all ingredients together and leave covered overnight. Strain before using.

CHICKEN ITALIAN STYLE

Time: 2–2½ hours
Temperature: 400–450°F
Serves: 10

1 x 4½–5 lb chicken
3 stalks celery
1 onion
1 clove garlic, crushed
sprig of marjoram

For sauce:
3 oz butter
3 good tablespoons (1½ oz)
   plain flour
3 cups chicken stock

2 teaspoons salt
1 lb mushrooms
2 oz butter
1 lb spaghetti

1 cup cream or top of milk
1½ cups grated tasty cheese
1 tablespoon brandy
salt and pepper

Place chicken in a large saucepan with two pints water, add the celery, quartered onion, garlic, marjoram and salt. Heat to simmering point and cook gently for 1½-2 hours until tender. When cooked, allow to cool. Skin the chicken, remove the meat and cut into cubes. Skim fat from stock and reduce to 3 cups by simmering with lid off. Remove mushroom stalks, wipe and slice caps if large. Sauté in melted butter. Lower spaghetti gradually into a large saucepan of boiling salted water. Boil with lid off for 12-15 minutes. Although softened when cooked, spaghetti should not be flabby and gelatinous.

To make Sauce: Melt the butter, add flour and allow it to bubble a little. Remove from the heat and add 1 cup of hot chicken stock. Stir well until smooth. Add remainder of stock and return to heat. Cook until thickened, stirring all the time. Add the cream or top of milk. Stir in half the cheese and the brandy. Add salt and pepper to taste. Place half the spaghetti in a greased ovenproof casserole, cover with the chicken and the mushrooms. Pour over half the cheese sauce. Top with remainder of spaghetti and sauce. Sprinkle remaining grated cheese on top. Bake in a hot oven for 30 minutes or until browned. Serve hot.

GREEK MARROW SALAD

Time: 30 minutes
Serves: 10

2 lb marrow
1 bunch spring onions or
   chives
$\frac{1}{4}$ cup olive oil

juice of 1 lemon
$\frac{1}{2}$ teaspoon salt
pepper

Choose young marrow in which the seeds have not yet hardened. Peel thinly and cut in $\frac{1}{2}$-inch slices. Do not remove seeds or pith. Poach gently in salted water until soft and translucent. Drain. Slice spring onions finely and sprinkle between layers of marrow in a serving dish. Pour over a dressing made by shaking the olive oil, lemon juice, salt and pepper together in a screw-top jar. Allow to marinate at least 1 hour before serving.

PIQUANT SALAD

Time: 20 minutes
Serves: 10

4 capsicums (peppers)
1 head of celery
4 red skinned apples
1 onion

4 large tomatoes, skinned
1 cup French Dressing (see
page 54)

Wash and dry the capsicums, celery and apples. Peel the onion. Cut capsicums in halves, remove seeds and membrane, slice flesh into $\frac{1}{4}$-inch slices. Cut celery into $\frac{1}{2}$-inch pieces. Do not peel the apples but remove cores and cut into cubes about the same size as the celery. Chop the onion finely. Mix capsicum, celery, apple and onion altogether. Add the tomatoes, cut into wedges. Toss prepared ingredients in French Dressing and serve chilled.

APRICOT WHIP

Serves: 10

2½ lb apricots
castor sugar to taste
2 tablespoons brandy
½ pint cream
3 egg whites

2 scant tablespoons (1 oz)
    sugar
extra whipped cream and
    angelica, for decoration

Halve and stone the apricots and steam them over hot
water until tender. Drain off any liquid and sieve the
fruit or purée in an electric blender. Add castor sugar
to taste and mix in the brandy. Leave to cool. Whip the
cream. Whisk the egg whites stiffly and add the sugar
gradually while beating. Combine with the cream and
gently fold into the apricot purée. Pile into dishes and
chill. Decorate with extra whipped cream and strips
of angelica.

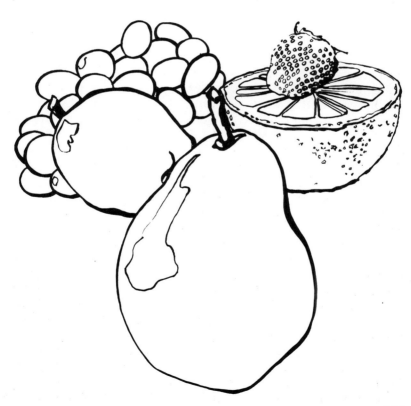

BARBECUE

Gerry Kearney

Simplicity is the key to barbecuing and portable barbecues provide the answer to the whims of the weather, making it easy to transfer operations at will to meet the challenge of sun, wind or rain. After many years of trial and error I have evolved a design which is genuinely portable, quickly assembled and quickly taken to pieces, that will stack flat in very little space in the boot of a car. Perfect for the small family barbecue. Yet with three or four of the same basic units and one or two helpers, one can comfortably barbecue for a thousand or more people. The barbecues are built of steel sheeting and, when assembled, look like a box standing on 4 legs. The bottom is perforated with holes to provide up-draft. Charcoal is spread to a depth of about 2-inches in the bottom of the box. Scattered over this, 6-inches apart, are large pieces of charcoal soaked in deodorised kerosene. The bed of charcoal is given a good squirt all over with methylated spirits, a lighted match is thrown in and the result is an instant fire.

Unlike a gas or electric oven, a barbecue does not come equipped with a convenient switch to adjust and control the heat, but it is just as important to do this if you do not want food cooked to a cinder on the outside and raw inside. Once

104

the fire is evenly alight I control the temperature with a hose fitted with a valve for a fine spray of water. This simple, but instant, accurate method of controlling heat opens the way to a whole new range of potential barbecue fare beyond the more usual steak, sausages and chops. It enables one to barbecue such delicate morsels as green prawns, Tasmanian scallops, mushrooms and other delicacies, knowing they will be tasty and juicy.

To handle small pieces of food quickly and in quantity, I use two pieces of equipment. A hairpin-shaped stainless steel skewer, about 30-inches long. One end is pointed and the other is made into a handle. Secondly, a smaller hairpin-shaped skewer, about 5-inches long. Food is threaded onto the small skewers which are in turn threaded onto the large skewers and placed over the fire. While cooking delicate food, the skewers must be turned frequently. The chef stands on the up-wind side of the fire, turning the skewers. When the food is cooked, the skewers with food are slipped off the larger skewers onto trays from which guests, armed with paper serviettes, help themselves—no plates, knives, forks, tables or chairs are required.

STEAK

Steak is the most popular barbecue food. There are three varieties which are delicious for barbecuing—rump, sirloin and fillet, in that order. Rather than cutting rump steak into individual portions and cooking these separately, it is better to cook large slices, 1-2-inches thick and then cut the cooked steak in serving portions. Rump steak is also excellent for kebabs, 1-inch cubes of steak alternating with pieces of onion, tomato and capsicum. Sirloin steak may be used in the same way as rump. However it needs to be carefully trimmed and all gristle removed. Alternatively, a whole sirloin may be barbecued over a slow fire, turning every few minutes. Cut into slices and served with vegetables, it is much tastier than the same meat cooked in an oven. Fillet steak should be well trimmed and barbecued whole.

One of the arts of barbecuing meat is to keep the juices in, not use them to feed the fire. Keep the meat a reasonable distance from the glowing coals (10-16-inches) and turn every few minutes. This keeps the juices running back and forth in the meat, away from the heat, and you will find the steak is juicy when it is served.

CHOPS

To barbecue chops, follow the same general rules as for steak but trim off all surplus fat. For something deliciously different, have your butcher cut through the bones of a loin of lamb, without severing the meat. Stuff fresh mint leaves in the creases between the chops. When cooked, the meat should be pink and full of juices and have a subtle flavour of mint.

Variations: Stuff lamb with apricots soaked in marsala, or fois gras instead of mint. Individual chops may have a pocket cut in the side and be stuffed in the same way.

SAUSAGES

Sausages should be parboiled for 5-10 minutes in boiling water before barbecuing. They should be turned frequently while barbecuing. Slit the sausages lengthways when cooked and place 2 or 3 cold oysters inside. It is a delicious combination, the contrast of hot and cold brings out the flavour.

CHICKEN

Chickens can be cut into small pieces, or, better still, partially boned and then chopped. Combined with small pieces of bacon, chicken makes very tasty kebabs. Rather than cook a whole chicken it is quicker to halve the birds first. As with steak, the secret is to retain the juices, and the method is a slow fire with frequent turning. Chickens have their own fat and no basting is needed.

SUCKING PIG

For barbecuing, a sucking pig should be under 20 lb.
Cut down the centre and score the legs. Rub the skin
with plenty of salt to give a crisp crackling. Owing to
its size, a pig must be cooked further away from the
fire, but with the thicker part nearest the fire. This may
be achieved by placing each half in a stainless wire
basket which hangs from a tall tripod over the
barbecue. Turn frequently, and allow more cooking
time on the bony side, too much on the other side will
burn the skin and ruin the crackling.

FISH

Large fish such as snapper, fresh Canadian salmon or
jewfish may be barbecued in wire baskets, turning
frequently. No basting is needed, but when cooked and
ready to slice, brush the fish with clarified butter and
lemon juice and season with salt and pepper. Small fish
may be threaded on stainless steel skewers for
barbecuing. However, it is safest to cook these in wire
baskets placed flat over the fire, closer to the heat.
Serve basted with clarified butter and lemon juice and
season with salt and pepper.

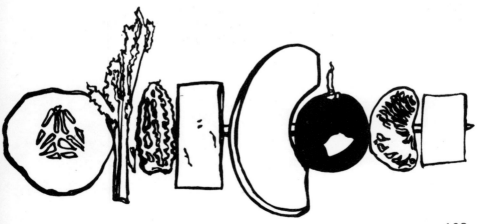

KEBABS

The possible combinations of ingredients when making
kebabs are limited only by one's imagination.
Here are a few suggestions that will be popular.
Chicken livers and mushrooms wrapped in bacon.
Kidney, onion and tomato wrapped in bacon.
Scallop and banana or mushroom wrapped in bacon.
Cubes of steak, onion, capsicum and tomato.
Pork and pineapple.
Lamb and apricot.
Chicken pieces and bacon.

VEGETABLES

Old potatoes are best when baked in the oven, then
threaded on skewers and finished over the barbecue.
Onions can be cooked in the same way. Tomatoes are
first spiked on small skewers then threaded on the
large skewers. And for something different, try
bananas in their skins, threaded on skewers and
cooked until the skins are black and bursting.

FRUIT

Flambéed fruit is a delicious finale at a barbecue.
Pineapple, peaches and strawberries are all ideal.
Skewer a whole pineapple and place over the fire until
it is warmed through, peel and cut into chunks. Place
chunks on a metal tray, add brown sugar and rum,
warm over the fire again, ignite and serve. Or take
fresh freestone peaches, halve them and remove the
stone, fill with brown sugar and rum or brandy.
Place on wire mesh over the fire and cook, then spread
on a metal tray, add some more rum or brandy and
ignite. With strawberries, place on a metal tray, add
brown sugar and rum or brandy, heat over barbecue,
ignite and shake well.

HAANGI

Con O'Leary

A shallow pit is scooped out of the ground, lawn turf being first cut out for later replacement if one is in a suburban setting. In Maori maraes (communal meeting places) special areas are set aside for the Haangi pits, handy to, but screened off from the meeting house. The circular pit need be no more than 10-inches deep and 4-feet in diameter to prepare a meal for up to 30 people. Pits up to 20-feet in diameter have been discovered and must have been capable of feeding several thousand people. Such large pits are about (18-inches deep. A solid stack of dense, hot-burning wood (manuka, tea-tree, rata and maire are popular) is then built over the pit. Heavy pieces of wood are placed at angles across and then the stack built up from kindling to form a solid platform on which the stones may be placed. The purpose of this is to concentrate the heat on the stones and to prevent any falling through prematurely. The stones used must be volcanic or porous, about half a football is a handy size, though some can be smaller. These are put on the wood stack, which is then set alight and left to burn for about an hour. When the stones are sitting on the embers the charred ends of timber are removed and the stones evenly spread through the pit. The stones should give off a blast of heat. While the stones are firing, food preparations are completed and baskets of food and a supply of water are at hand.

Joints of meat are first tossed onto the hot stones and quickly turned to singe or grill, sealing in the meat juices. All the meat is prepared in this way. Poultry, particularly mature or game birds, may be parboiled before placing in the Haangi. Meat is placed directly fat side down on the hot stones. Poultry is placed nearer the sides. Next, root vegetables are placed on top of the meat —kumera (sweet potato), potato, parsnip or turnip.

110

Pumpkin, laid skin down, sweet corn or squash may then be added and any green vegetables placed on top of these. Today, root vegetables and pumpkin are placed in a wire netting basket and vegetables such as cauliflower or cabbage are placed on top of these in a muslin bag. Poultry and suckling pigs may be placed in whole, other meats are usually cut into joints. Fresh water or salt water fish or shellfish may supplement the meat. Shellfish or eel may be placed on top so that their juices drip down to flavour the foods below. Shellfish may also be placed in baskets or an eel wrapped in cabbage leaves to retain the juices while cooking. In the latter case one can peel the skin off with the cabbage leaves or eat the preparation whole. Maoris generally prefer meat with the bone left in. Dried shark, once popular for flavouring Haangi food, does not seem as popular today. Water is quickly splashed onto the stones and food.

Baskets used in Haangi are made of woven flax and traditionally a strip of woven flax was placed around the edges and flax mats placed on top. Alternatively, certain species of fern which will not affect the flavour are used. Outside cabbage leaves can also be used. Clean muslin or linen may replace any of these but while the Maori might use washed flour sacks or tablecloths, nothing associated with the tapu of the body such as clothing or bed sheets may be used. Clean sacks are placed over the top and the earth shovelled back on. The Haangi must be constantly watched to prevent any steam escaping.

In the Haangi the fat melts and burns on the embers and stones. Smoke seeps through the Haangi giving the food a smoky taste often relished as the authentic Haangi flavour. This can be largely avoided by scraping out the embers or transferring the stones to a new pit. It can be completely avoided by putting the stones in two new pits, one for the meat and a few vegetables, which are roasted, the other for vegetables which are steamed. Very little water is added to the meat pit and quite a lot sprinkled in the vegetable pit. In a single pit the skilled Haangi maker will strike a balance between steamed and roasted meat and steamed vegetables.

The time taken for an average Haangi to cook varies from $1\frac{1}{2}$-$2\frac{1}{2}$ hours depending on the heat of the stones and the amount of food. Game meats, wild pork or venison might be placed in a Haangi and left overnight. Normal catering calculations can be used but as Haangi meat is usually exceptionally tasty it is best to supply more than usual. The Haangi is a very efficient method of catering for large gatherings but can also provide an enjoyable and different meal for a small family. Men do most of the cooking, generally preparing the meat and supervising the Haangi itself. Women prepare vegetables and other foods both for the Haangi or by other methods. Haangi food is often accompanied by boiled vegetables, particularly puha (native sow-thistle) or wild watercress. Boiling used to be accomplished by plunging hot stones into containers but became more efficient and popular with the introduction of metal pots. The Maori prefers green vegetables (puha, watercress or cabbage) boiled with meat such as pork bones, beef flank or fresh beef brisket. Huahua (preserved foods) such as preserved pigeons are great delicacies. The native pigeon is usually not cleaned so that the flavour of the wildberries it has been eating permeates the flesh. Cooked, or preserved whole, it is broken open by the thumbs, allowing the stomach to fall out in a ball and be cast away. Fish may also be fried, smoked, boiled or served raw with chopped

112

haangi

onions. Sometimes a fish, such as a trout, is quickly grilled by running it onto a stake which is then thrust into the ground on which the fire is burning. Certain clays can be used to pack around a gutted but unscraped fish. The damp clay forms a cast or shell, in the embers of the fire, which is easily knocked off, taking with it scales and skin, leaving clean, cooked flesh. Maori bread almost invariably accompanies a good Haangi. Round, flat loaves made from flour, water and home-grown potato yeast, cooked in the embers, in a camp oven or a range.

Modern variations include the use of aluminium foil in wrapping ingredients. One marae has dispensed with earth, placing hot stones in a circular concrete pit, which is covered by a steel cannister with a pressure gauge. But when individuals band together for a Haangi such modern developments are usually spurned, as men enjoy the traditional method and vie with one another for the authentic flavour. Great shame descends on one, whose Haangi is opened to disclose partially cooked meat. This seldom happens and the joy of uncovering a Haangi can be almost as great as the pleasure of eating it.

The central feature of Maori cooking is the Haangi or earth oven, which uses a steaming-roasting process. Now an important feature of New Zealand's national social life, to the extent of being popularly if inaccurately known as 'the New Zealand barbecue', the Haangi is commonly used for family meals, football socials (where a pig and a sack of potatoes accompany a hogshead of ale), to feasts for visiting notables, including royalty, where an amazing variety of delicious foods are prepared together by this single process.

wine and cheese party

WINE AND CHEESE PARTY

Frank Margan

There is a saying amongst the wine merchants of France, 'Buy on the apple and sell on the cheese'. It is a simple truth that the clean taste of an apple leaves the palate very sensitive to any faults in wine. On the other hand the fullness, the richness, even the sometimes cloying character of cheese can mask the palate and make all wine taste good.

Wine and Cheese Parties are tremendously popular for a number of reasons—the simple pleasure of the party itself, the ease and economy of the party, and the simple matching of the two great passions, wine and food. In fact, there is a certain affinity between wine and cheese and the bread that goes with it. They are all the products of a fermentation process. Traditionally, red wine was served with most cheeses but there are no rules about this. There are many new taste combinations to be discovered by drinking various white table wines with certain cheeses, even a sweet white table wine with certain varieties. A Wine and Cheese Party can be an economical or expensive occasion, one can purchase inexpensive flagon table wines and serve them with a Cheddar type cheese, available at any store, or one can serve more expensive wines with a vast range of full flavoured to delicate textured cheeses. Another popular idea is a 'bring a bottle and a cheese' party where the guests select their own cheese and the wine that will best accompany it and bring both items along. On an occasion like this, the wines may be masked and the purchaser of each bottle calls for comments from the other guests.

Hints for giving a successful Wine and Cheese Party.

Preferably, each guest should have 2 glasses so that different wines may be compared.

Use stemmed wine glasses which are clear and unadorned and have a capacity of approximately 6-7 fl oz.

The glasses should only be half filled with wine, so that the bouquet of the wine can be trapped between the wine's surface and the rim of the glass.

It is not necessary to have a new glass for each wine. The same glass may be used, as long as it is rinsed with a little of the new wine which is poured into the glass and swilled around the sides before being emptied into a 'swill jug'.

You can estimate the amount of wine you should provide by calculating that each guest will consume approximately half a bottle of wine during a Wine and Cheese Party.

The wines should be mainly dry in style and you will require about 3 bottles of red, for every bottle of white wine.

Allow 2-3 oz cheese per person. Slices of savoury

flan or pizza may also be served.

The red wines should be served at room temperature and the white wines should be chilled.

The white wines—hock, riesling, Rhine riesling, chablis or white burgundy, need only 30 minutes in the refrigerator to bring them to the correct temperature. Wine is chilled most successfully in an ice bucket at the table and the wine in the frosted bucket makes an attractive table decoration.

The red wines—claret, burgundy or simply dry red, should be opened about 30 minutes before serving, giving them time to breathe and thus activating the bouquet of the wine and liberating its flavour.

The red wines are ideal with all cheeses and are essential with the stronger flavoured ones such as blue vein, camembert and the more piquant flavoured varieties.

With the softer, blander cheeses and those with a more delicate flavour such as edam and fetta, you might like to serve a full-flavoured white wine, in the white burgundy style.

You can experiment with the cheeses that are slightly sweet in flavour such as the French and Italian grape seed cheeses or Italian erbo cheese, by serving a sweeter flavoured wine such as a graves, or one of the spatlese or auslese varieties. The spatlese and auslese wines are made by picking the grapes very late in the season, when they are shrivelled by the sun, giving them a high sugar content. They are distinguished by a sweetish, very fruity taste on the front of the palate and should have a clean, dry finish. Served chilled, they can provide a new taste experience with a cheese that neither dominates or is dominated by them.

This is the important point to remember when serving all wines and foods, the flavours should complement, not override each other. The red wines provide their own guides as to the cheeses that should accompany them. The claret style of dry red is distinguished by volume of flavour and a dry, mouth-puckering astringency on the palate after the wine has been swallowed. The burgundy type of red wine is softer, fruitier and seemingly smoother in flavour, with a softer finish than the claret style. The sharper, fuller flavoured cheeses of the blue vein variety, the stronger Cheddars and gorgonzolas complement the astringent claret styles of wine. The softer, more delicately flavoured cheeses of the camembert, brie, gruyère and Leicester styles complement the fruitier flavours of the burgundy type of red wine.

PIZZALINAS

Tiny winey pizza pies, ideal to serve with red wine at a Wine and Cheese Party.

Time: 25 minutes
Temperature: 300–325°F
Serves: 6–8

1 oz butter
4 tablespoons olive oil
4 oz bacon or salt pork, finely chopped
1 onion, finely chopped
1 carrot, finely chopped
8 oz finely minced beef
1 strip of lemon rind
4 tablespoons tomato paste
½ pint beef stock or water and beef stock cube

¼ pint dry red or white wine
1 bay leaf
pinch of ground nutmeg
½ teaspoon salt
freshly ground black pepper
6–8 slices bread, cut from round loaf
grated Parmesan cheese, for serving

Heat butter and oil in a saucepan and sauté bacon, onion and carrot for 5 minutes. Stir in minced beef and cook until browned. Add lemon rind, tomato paste, beef stock, wine, bay leaf, nutmeg, salt and pepper. Bring to the boil and simmer, covered, for 30 minutes, stirring occasionally. Remove lemon rind and bay leaf and simmer, uncovered, for a further 30 minutes. The sauce should be thick and rich. Spread on slices of bread. Place on baking trays and sprinkle with Parmesan cheese. Bake in a slow oven until bubbly, approximately 25 minutes. Serve immediately.

QUICHE LORRAINE WITH WINE

A wine flavoured Quiche Lorraine to serve with chilled white wine.

Time: 45–50 minutes
Temperature: 375–400°F
   reducing to 300–325°F
Serves: 6

Pastry:
1 cup (4 oz) plain flour
2 oz butter
1 egg yolk

squeeze of lemon juice
2–3 teaspoons cold water
$\frac{1}{2}$ teaspoon salt

For filling:
8 oz Swiss cheese, grated
2 onions, thinly sliced
3 eggs
$\frac{1}{2}$ pint cream, whipped

$\frac{1}{4}$ cup riesling
$\frac{1}{2}$ clove garlic, crushed
$\frac{1}{4}$ teaspoon freshly ground
   black pepper
$\frac{1}{4}$ teaspoon ground nutmeg

To Make Pastry: Sieve flour into mixing bowl. Rub butter into flour with fingertips until the mixture resembles fine breadcrumbs. Mix egg yolk, lemon juice, water and salt together, add to flour and mix with a round bladed knife until the mixture holds together. Cover and allow to stand in refrigerator for 30 minutes. Roll pastry out thinly on a lightly floured board and line an 8-inch flan ring. Trim edges of flan and prick base with a fork. Line inside of flan ring with a circle of greased greaseproof paper and sprinkle with dried beans or peas. Bake in a moderately hot oven for 15-20 minutes until pastry is cooked but not brown, remove paper and beans.

To Make Filling and finish Flan: Place cheese in pastry flan, sprinkle with sliced onions. Beat together the eggs, cream, wine, garlic and pepper. Pour into the pastry flan and sprinkle lightly with nutmeg. Bake in a slow oven for 30 minutes or until custard is set. Serve with chilled riesling.

ACKNOWLEGMENTS

The editor would like to thank the following for their help and co-operation in the preparation of and photography for this book:

Babette Hayes for photography design

The following contributors who prepared food for photographs:

Enid Wells
Elah Lowe
Louis Ferguson
Gretta Anna Teplitzky
Daphne Eilers
Gerry Kearney
Con O'Leary and Maori students

Dairy Board for cheese
Incorporated Agencies Pty. Ltd. for tableware
Len Evans for wine
Air New Zealand
Ansett Airlines of Australia

123

INDEX

124

127

198